Edith Sylla
1997

law of nature   82 ff

Omnipotence, Covenant, & Order

OTHER BOOKS BY FRANCIS OAKLEY

The Political Thought of Pierre d'Ailly

Council over Pope?

The Medieval Experience

The Western Church in the Later Middle Ages

Natural Law, Conciliarism, and Consent
in the Late Middle Ages

Editor, with Daniel O'Connor

Creation: The Impact of an Idea

Omnipotence, Covenant, & Order

AN EXCURSION IN THE HISTORY OF
IDEAS FROM ABELARD TO LEIBNIZ

BY FRANCIS OAKLEY

Cornell University Press
ITHACA AND LONDON

First published 1984 by Cornell University Press.
Published in the United Kingdom by Cornell University Press Ltd., London

International Standard Book Number 0–8014–1631–0
Library of Congress Catalog Card Number 83–45945

Printed in the United States of America

Librarians: Library of Congress cataloging information appears on the last page of the book.

The paper in this book is acid-free and meets the guidelines for permanence and durability of the Committee on Production Guidelines for Book Longevity of the Council on Library Resources.

To
Deirdre
Christopher
Timothy
Brian

Contents

8   *Contents*

Preface

Over the course of the past decade and a half, as meta-historical and methodological debates have come to disturb the commonsensical dogmatic slumbers of historians in general and intellectual historians in particular, I have been repeatedly struck by two things. First, the unfortunate and widening gulf between the work of those on the one hand whose creative energies are fully engaged in the actual doing of history and the arguments of those on the other whose concerns focus almost exclusively on the methodological issue—now almost a subspecialty in its own right. Second, the casual way in which those interested in exploring or promoting the newer approaches to intellectual history so often brush to one side the claims Arthur O. Lovejoy made, now almost half a century ago, for his own approach to the history of ideas. Those claims were neither overweening nor monopolistic, and in his *Great Chain of Being* Lovejoy succeeded in demonstrating the efficacy and power of his chosen approach in coming to terms at least with certain types of intellectual phenomena. And while I have long been persuaded that the overall picture of European intellectual history outlined in his classic work calls in some measure for qualification and revision, I have been equally convinced that that process of qualification can best be promoted not by the abandonment but by the continued exploitation of the methodological approach he himself pioneered.

For some years, then, it was my intention, should an appropriate occasion present itself, to produce a short study combining methodological prescription with concrete historical exemplification in such a way as to engineer a significant qualification of Lovejoy's vision of European intellectual history while at the same time (indeed, by the act of so doing) vindicating the validity, efficacy, and fruitfulness of his improperly maligned approach to intellectual history. A happy invitation from Oberlin College to deliver the Mead-Swing lectures there afforded me, in the autumn of 1981, the appropriate occasion. And the following pages derive from those lectures.

After an opening chapter devoted to methodological issues in general and a defense of Lovejoy's approach in particular, I proceed to use that approach in the three chapters remaining to trace from the twelfth to the seventeenth century the history of a theme on which pivoted, during those centuries, a coherent scheme of things contrasting sharply with the picture evoked by the notion of the great chain of being but rivaling it by its own imaginative force. The theme in question, familiar enough nowadays to historians of late-medieval philosophy and theology but to few others besides, is the distinction between the absolute and ordained or ordinary powers of God—and, by frequently invoked analogy, of popes, emperors, and kings. The scheme: the vision of an order—natural, moral, salvational, political—grounded not in the very nature of things but rather in will, promise, and covenant. Only if historians recognize, I argue, that radically different conceptions of order jostle side by side in the texts confronting them will the perplexities generated by some segments of early modern legal, theological, and scientific thinking be successfully dissipated.

It gives me pleasure to thank the members of the Mead-Swing committee and the many other faculty members and students—not least among them Marcia Colish and Grover Zinn—whose numerous kindnesses made my visit to Oberlin so stimulating and so very enjoyable. The bulk of the writing was completed amid the incomparable surroundings of the Institute for Advanced Study, Princeton, where it was my good fortune, with the help of a fellowship from the National Endowment for the Humanities, to spend the academic year 1981–82 as a member of the School of Historical Studies. And I owe a special debt of gratitude to my colleagues in the political theory seminar there (as well as to my colleagues in the Department of History at Williams College) for giving me the opportunity to try out on them the line of argument pursued in the opening chapter.

Among the other debts I have incurred in the course of writing and preparing the manuscript I gratefully acknowledge the award of a grant from the Class of 1900 Fund at Williams and the excellent work of Donna Chenail and Rosemary Lane of our faculty secretarial office. But in complex and less direct ways my indebtednesses run deeper and reach much further into the past. In one or another of its dimensions, my preoccupation with Lovejoy and the covenantal theme has been with me for many years. And it is intertwined in my mind, in a fashion too familiar to be altogether incongruous, with happy recollections of familial distractions reaching back to the days when my children were no more than toddlers. So now that (inexplicably) they have grown, it seems no more than fitting that I should dedicate this little book to them, with deep affection and a good deal of parental pride.

F. O.

Williamstown, Massachusetts

Omnipotence, Covenant, & Order

Chapter 1

AGAINST THE STREAM:
IN PRAISE OF LOVEJOY

Methodology can only be self-reflection
on the means which have proven to be
valuable in actual research.
                              —Max Weber

I

For historians, these are truly, it seems, "the best of times and the worst of times, the age of wisdom and the age of foolishness, the epoch of belief and the epoch of incredulity, the season of light, the season of darkness, the spring of hope, the winter of despair." No one possessed of even a nodding acquaintance with the development of historical studies since World War II can fail to be impressed by the speed with which the profession has expanded worldwide, the energy with which it has opened up new fields of inquiry, the openness it has shown toward new investigative techniques drawn largely from the social sciences, the exuberant creativity manifest in the unassimilable flow of articles, essays, monographs, and books deluging the pages and review

columns of the growing number of journals and periodicals
devoted to matters historical.[1] Historians themselves, however, are sharply divided in their appraisal of all this activity,
arguing with one another about the wisdom of so impetuous
an expansion, disagreeing about the impact of so explosive an
energy, the desirability of so promiscuous a productivity.

About the facts, admittedly, there is little room for dispute. The years since the war have witnessed what has been,
in effect, the completion of the process whereby historical
studies have passed from amateur hands into those of univer-
sity-trained and -based professionals. That process, which began in Germany in the late eighteenth and early nineteenth
centuries and spread thence by the end of the latter century
to the other Western countries, has since become global in
scale, and it is possible to chart its progress by the foundings
of successive national and regional professional journals. Just
as the second half of the nineteenth century saw the *Histo-
rische Zeitschrift* founded in Germany in 1859, the *Revue
historique* in France in 1876, the *English Historical Review*
in 1886, and the *American Historical Review* in 1895, so the
last few years have seen the foundation, for example, of the
Revista de historia (1950) in Brazil, of the *Historia mexicana*
(1951), of the *Journal of the Historical Society of Nigeria*
(1956), and of *Afrika Zamani, Revue d'histoire africaine*,
published since 1974 by the (Francophone) Association of
African Historians.

While this process has brought with it the diffusion
worldwide of the documentary techniques, interpretive canons, and intense preoccupation with the nation state characteristic of European historiography in the early twentieth
century, in its wake has swiftly followed the transmission
along the newly established lines of professional commu-
nication of the first tremors of discontent with the constrict-
ing and stultifying effects of that preoccupation and those
canons and techniques, once they had come to be sanctioned

by use and hallowed by success. Though felt also during the 1930s and 1940s in England and North America, that discontent found its quintessential expression from 1929 onward in the work of the so-called *Annales* school of historians, associated with the journal of the same name and with that veritable holy trinity of French historiography: Lucien Febvre, Marc Bloch, and Fernand Braudel. Some broad, general dispositions united the *Annalistes* with their fellow malcontents in other countries—a certain disdain for the traditional historical narrative of political events and a correlative preference for a more ecumenic analytic mode, a suspicion of conclusions drawn from the surface play of rational deliberation and conscious human choice, a determination to penetrate beneath such epiphenomena, to chart the subterranean flow of irrational motivations, and to map the impersonal but enduring geologic structures (ecological, demographic, social, economic) that shape across time the destiny of man. A preoccupation also with collective mass behavior rather than the thinking, willing, or striving of individuals and a concomitant willingness to turn to the social sciences for the conceptual tools and analytic techniques alone capable of rendering such mass phenomena susceptible to historical investigation. All of these dispositions, by a revolution that has been neither quiet nor limited to Western Europe and North America, have come over the past two decades to characterize the professional historical establishment at large.

Hence "the historiographical whirlwind" that has been said of recent years to have "transformed" the profession[2]—the fascination with psychohistory, the impact of studies in historical demography, the growing interest in family history in particular and the huge surge of work in social history in general, above all the intoxicating discovery that Gray's "short and simple annals of the poor" prove on closer inspection rarely to have been simple and promise almost never, it seems, to be short. Hence, too, the confident promotion of

quantitative techniques, the obsessive talk about writing history "from the bottom up", the persistent patter of references
to grids, coordinates, episteme, *mentalité*, "thick description," *la longue durée*, paradigms, Cliometrics, the "new
economic history," the "new social history," the "new political history," and even, and not surely without a touch of
arrogance, the "new history" *tout court*.

For some, and especially those seeking their intellectual
fortunes in the brawling frontier settlements of the new historiography, this transformation of their chosen discipline
has been a vitalizing and truly exhilarating one, generating
intimations, if not indeed of immortality, at least of manifest
destiny, rich with promise for a millennial reintegration of
history with all the social sciences and for "the beginning of
a true 'science humaine.' "[3] Even so acute (and chastened) an
observer of the historiographic scene as Lawrence Stone can
describe the years since 1940, "together with the forty years
before the First World War," as "the most fruitful and creative period in the whole history of the profession."[4] Others—such as Jacques Barzun and Gertrude Himmelfarb, who
have mounted a vigorous frontal attack no less on the central
claims being made for the "new history" than on the excesses of some of its quantifying or psychohistorical practitioners[5]—others, however, are not so sure. And none less so,
I would suggest, than the intellectual historians, whose primary concern it has been to explore the concepts and beliefs
of the past, formal and informal, articulate and inarticulate,
but who have now seen their subject shunted to one side,
consigned to uncertain escort duties on the outer flanks of
the professional flotilla of disciplinary subspecialties, cheat-
ed of that "flagship role" to which in North America it had
aspired during the 1940s and 1950s.[6] Indeed, the very inten-
sity of their fear that intellectual history is threatened with
"reduction . . . to a function of social history" and social
problems elevated "to the status of the only truly significant

historical problems"[7] suggests something of a loss of sub-disciplinary nerve, a gloomy sense, perhaps, that there is something after all to the claims of the "new historians," a concession at least to the rumor that theirs is the wave of the future, a disposition, accordingly, to acquiesce in the pessimistic judgment recently handed down to the effect that "intellectual history has had a brief but glorious past, suffers a beleaguered present, and has no future."[8]

It would be easy enough to dismiss that judgment, and, in no small measure, proper to do so. If the past of intellectual history may well be claimed to have been glorious, it must certainly in America be conceded not only to have been brief but also to have been dogged by a good deal of robust skepticism. A hard-boiled political historian once derided its endeavor as "like trying to nail jelly to the wall."[9] In that derisive appraisal he was by no means alone. Nor, I suspect, would he be alone today. Again, if some of its practitioners may well perceive the future of intellectual history to be bleak, their actual behavior—as reflected in the percentages of dissertations produced, courses offered, articles written—appears to belie that fact. For, over the past twenty years, those percentages have held remarkably steady.[10] And if their present is in some degree indeed a beleaguered one, intellectual historians can now take heart. Relief, it seems, is in sight. For its undiscriminating social-scientism it is the "new history" itself that is now coming under criticism. "Warning signals are flying about threats of a new dogmatism and a new methodological scholasticism."[11] And they are being hoisted not by obdurate defenders of an obsolescent humanism, but by some of the "new historians" themselves. It is Lawrence Stone, after all, who now tells us that "quantification has not fulfilled the high hopes of twenty years ago," that "many historians now believe the culture of the group, and even the will of the individual" to be "potentially at least as important causal agents of change as the impersonal forces of material output and demographic growth," that "economic history and demographic determinism" have now been "undermined by a recognition of ideas, culture and individual will as independent variables."[12]

After tossing for many a long and restless night on their temporarily unfashionable subdisciplinary beds, intellectual historians can now begin, it seems, to sleep more soundly, secure in the knowledge that the esteem of their colleagues, of recent years so crushingly withheld from their endeavors, is now once more to be accorded to them. But not to all, it should be noted, for intellectual historians come in many shapes and sizes. And not in full measure, for certain types of investigation traditionally pursued under their aegis remain clearly unworthy of the profession's esteem. Not so history of collective *mentalités*, of course. Or history of the beliefs, feelings, values, and attitudes of the inarticulate masses. Or history, even, of the ideas of elites, provided that they are precisely situated in the social, intellectual, and linguistic contexts of their times. But history of ideas as it was so often pursued in the past by such as Meinecke and Cassirer, Lovejoy, Perry Miller, Passerin d'Entrèves, history of ideas concerned less with contextual factors of a social nature than with the logical analysis of ideas, of their reciprocal interaction or their internal development within an intellectual tradition or discipline, characterized sometimes by a desire to identify the patterns of thought unifying whole periods or societies and at others by a concern to trace the careers of ideas across large spans of time—history of ideas, so conceived, remains, it seems, under proscription. Indeed, we are assured that the very precondition for the novel interest of the "new history" in "trying to discover what was going on inside people's heads in the past" is nothing other than "the collapse of traditional intellectual history treated as a kind of paper-chase of ideas back through the ages" and usually ending up "with either Aristotle or Plato."[13]

Having set myself, however, the task of mounting precisely such a paper chase (and anyone who has undertaken this sort of task will readily concede its difficulty), having committed myself to an excursion in the history of ideas from the age of Abelard in the mid-twelfth century to that of Leibniz in the early eighteenth, I feel bound to share with you the sense, deeply felt, that the publication of any obituary for the genre is a trifle premature. Recognizing, moreover, that in undertaking that excursion I shall be striving against the historiographic stream, I feel bound also (while ruefully acknowledging the pertinence and sting of Max Weber's remarks about the "methodological pestilence" prevailing in his own discipline)[14] to take as my point of departure the nature of the history of ideas as well as the methodological criticisms and procedural complaints that have been lodged so very persistently against it.

II

Among historians such criticisms and complaints amount with striking frequency to little more than mutually reinforcing expressions of shared and fashionable distaste. Nonetheless they are susceptible of more rigorous formulation and are not lightly to be dismissed. Indeed, even if one limits oneself to viewpoints currently in vogue, one is forced to a gloomy concession of the range and complexity of the body of criticism already generated. That body may be said to fall into two major subgroupings, the first moral and political in inspiration, fairly homogeneous in texture, possessed of a certain plausible incoherence and of a considerable if surely waning influence, the second linguistic and philosophical in inspiration, intimidatingly various in texture, implausibly coherent (at least in some of its component parts), making a delayed but currently mounting impact.

The former need not detain us long. Though long predating the social and political turmoil of the 1960s, it was from the conditions of that era that it drew much of its appeal and it is now beginning to show its age. Attacking the work of the historians of ideas as " 'minority' history of the wrong kind—reflecting the values of élites rather than of downtrodden groups,"[15] it tended to reduce the history to the *sociology* of ideas, the conceptual creativity of original thinkers—literate, articulate, and usually emerging from the privileged strata of society—to the predictable ideology of their class, while at the same time failing to explain just why its own critical stance should not itself be categorized in comparable fashion as ideologically determined. At the same time, on another front, it either ignored the fact that some of the most deeply rooted and widely held of popular beliefs and values were themselves originally the contribution of individual creativity, or left itself defenseless against the charge that it smacked of a "patronizing humanitarianism" to suppose that the "masses who live in poverty should be properly concerned only with their poverty."[16]

The latter grouping of critical positions, those of linguistic and philosophical inspiration, is much more formidable of mien, a veritable cat's cradle of overlapping, entangled, and countervailing argumentation. If we are to make anything of it at all (for it comprehends some diametrically opposed intellectual commitments), we must break it down into two further subordinate subgroupings.

The first is French in origin, a complex series of intersecting ripples generated by the successive waves of intellectual fashion, structuralist and poststructuralist, which have broken over the Parisian cultural world since the decline of existentialism as the philosophical standard bearer in the late 1950s.[17] The principal impact of these intellectual tendencies, associated for the English-speaking world especially with the names of Claude Lévi-Strauss, Michel Foucault, Roland Barthes, and Jacques Derrida, has been on anthropology, psychoanalysis (French style, à la Jacques Lacan), linguistics, literary criticism, and, in some measure, philosophy—though in this last case essentially by incorporating it into another discipline. But the impact on history has been less, except directly via some of Foucault's writings and indirectly via the intense preoccupation of such poststructuralists as Barthes and Derrida with texts, their status, and strategies for reading them. That preoccupation has, at least for the past decade, been generating powerful harmonics among the theorists of literary criticism here in America, but it is only now beginning to catch the attention of the intellectual historians.[18]

In the case of Foucault—the Foucault, at least, of *Les Mots et les choses* and *L'Archéologie du savoir*—his contempt for the traditional history of ideas cannot even in charity be said to be ill concealed. It is a mode of inquiry that smacks, he says, of "simplemindedness," a "rather shopsoiled idea," one that only "conservative zeal" or nostalgia for the familiar history of one's childhood could lead one still to invoke. His own approach, his "archaeology of knowledge," amounts in effect, he insists, to "an abandonment of the history of ideas, a systematic rejection of its postulates and procedures." A rejection, that is to say, of its concern with thoughts or preoccupations concealed or revealed in written works, with the sources, context, or influence of those works, with the role of "creative subject" as their raison d'être, with the attempt "to restore what has been thought, wished, aimed at, experienced, desired by men in the very moment at which they expressed it in discourse."[19] As the name itself suggests, his own "archaeological description" claims to operate instead at another, more profound level, to search out the "fundamental codes" of cultures, those deep underlying structures, grounded in the very bedrock of human consciousness, indeed of language itself. And

it is employed in *The Order of Things* not to chart those
continuities across time so dear to the traditional historian of
ideas, but rather to map in synchronic fashion the networks
or grids of relationships that give unity to each of the four
great epistemes (or "epochs of epistemic coherence")[20] into
which the years since the later Middle Ages have fallen, and
to identify (though by no means to explain) the catastrophic
discontinuities that have separated them one from another.

   Although (along with Lévi-Strauss) Foucault is sometimes
depicted as sympathizing with the aspirations of the *Annales*
school, or as sharing with its founders a heritage deriving
from those old debates about the scientific status of the historical method that filled the pages of the *Revue de synthèse*
under the editorship of Henri Berr in the early decades of the
twentieth century,[21] it is not to be supposed that his discontent with the traditional goals and procedures of the history
of ideas has really much in common with theirs. It goes
much deeper and is fueled by sources alien to theirs—above
all, it seems, by Nietzsche, the first, he says, to wake us from
"the anthropological sleep,"[22] and (though less clearly) by
highly selective extrapolations from the structuralist linguistics deriving ultimately from Ferdinand de Saussure.[23] Tune
out the static generated by Foucault's beguiling patter of references to "the prose of the world," the "untamed, imperious
being of words," the "murmur of the ontological con-
tinuum," "the endless murmur of nature," the "silence" or,
alternatively, the "endless murmur" of the Unconscious,[24]
and one picks up the harsher tones of a much more uncompromising signal. Penetrate the incantatory opacity of his
prose and one catches glimpses of a far more threatening
vision. Foucault, we have been told, is "one of the great
historians or our time."[25] But we should not miss the fact
that his real target in these methodological works of his, the
true burden of his plaint, is not the failings of the traditional
history of ideas but the bankruptcy of history in general—

indeed, beyond history, that of the so-called human sciences as they have conventionally been comprehended and practiced. As Hayden White has put it, Foucault "writes 'history' in order to destroy it," regarding it "less as a 'method' or a 'mode of thought' than as a symptom of a peculiarly nineteenth-century malaise which originated in the discovery of the temporality of all things."[26] Like all the other human sciences, it remains trapped within its own "linguistic protocols," blind to the fact that such concepts as "man," "society," and "culture" refer "not to things, but to linguistic formulae" lacking any "specific referent in reality," blind also to the fact that the disciplinary strategies devised for the study of such concepts "are little more than abstractions of the rules of the language games that they represent."[27]

This being so, and Foucault having abandoned the traditional historiographic concern with the reality of the past as it actually happened, an attitude of prudent reserve may be recommended to any historian tempted to make use of his strictures in an attempt to bracket or downgrade the traditional goals and procedures of the history of ideas. And the same recommendation should be made, I believe, with even greater force to any intellectual historian beguiled, as some already are and more will surely be, by the promise of a more profound and less restrictively "documentary" reading of their textual sources which the textual strategies brilliantly promoted by such poststructuralists as Barthes and Derrida and eagerly oversold by some of their American admirers seem to hold out.

For here the burden of the Nietzschean perspective on language and knowledge—indeed, of Nietzschean "perspectivism" or relativism in general—is crushingly apparent.[28] Nietzsche had raised the question of the arbitrary nature of language and dismissed the notion of "the subject" as being no more than "a linguistic convenience."[29] In poststructuralist criticism that dismissal has, on linguistic or metalinguistic grounds, been extended and radicalized. The "death" or "disappearance" of the author is proclaimed to the point of absurdity,[30] and with it "the dearth of meaning."[31] Language is prior to meaning; it is "our Seigneur," and "the question of language" now "seems to lay siege on every side to the figure of man," that figure which, for Foucault after all, is "no more than a kind of rift in the order of things," a "new wrinkle in our knowledge,"[32] "The *I* that writes the text," says Barthes, "is never, itself, anything more than a paper *I*." The text itself, in turn, is "a stereophonic space," a "migration of meanings, the outcroppings of codes," the "*stereographic plurality* of the signifiers that weave it," assuring that it possesses "an *irreducible* plurality" of meanings, and allowing "no enunciative subject to hold the position of judge, teacher, analyst, confessor or decoder."[33]

And so on, the whole surrounded by a smoky, bewildering, and intimidating screen of terms, phrases, and distinctions—*langue et parole*, "intertextuality," *écriture*, "metaphysics of presence," "transcendental signified," "logocentrism," "desedimentation," *différance*, and so on—many of them of Saussurian or Heideggerian provenance or the product of Derrida's irrepressible proclivity for neologizing. But as one peers anxiously into the crowded gloom, it becomes increasingly clear that in its most extreme forms, at least, what is being urged by these thinkers is "a mode of reading which undermines . . . the possibility of understanding language as a medium of decidable meanings," and, even in its less extreme versions, one that in its thoroughgoing relativism or "perspectivism" "eventuates in a radical scepticism about our ability to achieve a correct interpretation."[34]

For some of our most innovative and provocative literary critics, oddly enough, this debilitating skepticism appears to pose no threat. Reading for them, they bravely assure us, is an *adventure* itself productive of the meanings it cannot be said to discover. It has become a "creative adventure in liberated interpretation,"[35] and we are subjected, accordingly, to a lot of bright talk about "strong" reading, "creative reading," "interpretation as joyful wisdom," as "joy in the midst of suffering"—a plethora of whistling, if you wish, in the encompassing Nietzschean dark.[36] But if there is some reason to doubt whether this will in the end turn out to be a truly viable option even for the literary critic, there is a good deal more reason to suspect that it is not an option with which *historians* can safely flirt and still remain recognizable as such. To respond with sympathy to E. D. Hirsch's insistence that "without the stable determinancy of meaning there can be no knowledge in interpretation, nor any knowledge in the many humanistic disciplines based upon textual interpretation," one does not have to be an old-fashioned historian of ideas.[37] It is enough, simply, to be a historian. Wittingly or unwittingly, these poststructuralist authors (for paradoxically, they expect that *they* will be taken as authors and that *their* intended meanings will be respected by the reader)[38] appear to have backed themselves into a philosophical cul-de-sac. And it remains very much open to question whether without leaving it they can do much more, however interestingly or provocatively, than rummage around in the accumulated intellectual debris that the winds of chance and the traffic of time have deposited therein. On that question, or so I would urge, the verdict is not yet in.[39]

Given this fact, I might be expected with some relief to extend a warm welcome to those other critics for whom the notion of authorship happily poses no problem—those, in effect, who rather than leave the reader adrift on "the communal sea of linguicity"[40] strive to anchor determinate textual meaning in the firm seabed of authorial intentionality. And indeed I do welcome that general approach. But the sharp edge of my pleasure is blunted somewhat by the fact that numbered among its proponents are those who form the second subgrouping of methodologists who, on linguistic and philosophical grounds, have wished to challenge the traditional goals and procedures of the history of ideas. This subgroup, composed of J. G. A. Pocock, John Dunn, and Quentin Skinner, is moved in part by the general preoccupation with problems of language shown by the analytical philosophers of the English-speaking world, especially by Wittgenstein's stress on the importance of studying the actual use to which propositions are put in any particular "language game" and by J. L. Austin's and John Searle's later development of speech-act theory.[41] But its members are moved also, perhaps more, by the heavy freight of mythology, fiction, conceptual confusion, distortion, absurdity, even, generated by the ahistorical or inadequately historical goals and procedures that they regard as characteristic in general of the history of ideas, and in truly crippling degree of the history of political thought as it is traditionally pursued. Hence their anxiety to impose some sort of limit on the dangerously broad range of conceivable interpretations to which the writings of the past lend themselves. Hence, too, their concern with reconstructing historically the linguistic and cognitive contexts of past utterances. As Dunn puts it: "If a statement is considered in a fully open context, its meaning may be any lexically possible set of colligations of the uttered propositions. . . . The problem of interpretation is always the problem of closing the context. [And] what closes the context in actuality is the intention (and, much more broadly, the experiences) of the speaker."[42]

All three critics, though in differing degree,[43] share this preoccupation with authorial intentionality and with contextual strategies for identifying that intentionality—such as asking "what an author, in writing at the time he did write, for the audience he intended to address, could in practice have been intending to communicate by the utterance of [a] . . . given utterance."[44] But it is Skinner that pursues that line of thought most systematically and with a truly admirable degree of tenacity and precision. In so doing, he argues that "the key to excluding unhistorical meanings must lie in limiting our range of descriptions of any given text to those which the author himself might in principle have avowed," "that the key to understanding the actual historical meanings of a text must lie in recovering the complex intentions of the author in writing it," and that the high road to the recovery of that author's "primary intentions" lies in a firm grasp of what Austin called the "illocutionary force" of his utterances—that is, "what he may have been intending to do simply in writing in a certain way."[45]

So far, so good. Though not unaware of the fact that this approach is open to criticism, in some measure on highly technical grounds,[46] I find myself in broad sympathy with its goals and grateful for the protection it affords against both the excesses of poststructuralism and the reductionism sometimes exhibited by the sociologists of knowledge. The more so, indeed, in that Skinner, some of his critics to the contrary, does not claim that the recovery of an author's intentions constitutes the interpreter's entire task, but rather that it must be among that interpreter's tasks. The more so, too, in that he now emphasizes that "to be concerned with a writer's intentions in this way" does not mean that "we must be prepared to accept any statements which the writer himself may make about his own intentions as a final authority on the question of what he was doing in a particular work."[47] The more so, again, in that he has striven to make clear, responding to his critics, that his stress on contextualism does not proscribe the recognition in an author of innovation and creativity, that he would not deny to an author the aim of extending, subverting, or in some other way altering "a prevailing set of accepted conventions and attitudes."[48]

My sympathy becomes somewhat strained, however,

when to the listing of the heinous faults traditionally characteristic of the history of ideas (in Skinner's case a veritable
syllabus of errors compiled with a degree of polemical zeal
about which he himself now concedes a twinge of mild re-
gret)[49] is appended the conclusion that the methodology for
the history of ideas proposed by Lovejoy and his school—that
of concentrating on the idea itself as a unit and of tracing its
morphology across time—not only is prone to produce the
type of "conceptual morass" that Dunn deplores,[50] but is
itself misguided, is wrong in principle, "rests on a fundamental philosophic mistake."[51] As Skinner says, for it is he that
is totally explicit on this matter, "My concern . . . is not
empirical but conceptual: not to insist that such histories
can sometimes go wrong, but that they can never go right."[52]

His reasons for drawing this disconcerting conclusion he
states with an uncharacteristic lack of precision, and I must
limit myself to proffering two comments on the matter. Both
concern, appropriately enough, text, context, and the matter
of authorial intentionality, but the texts in question now,
and the intentions involved, are those of Skinner and Lovejoy
themselves. First, Skinner. Although the claims he makes are
applied on a broader front, he himself has testified to the fact
that the intellectual context of his methodological enterprise
was the way in which the history specifically of *political
thought* was being written, and it was, in fact, from the
crimes, real or alleged, of the historians of political thought
that he compiled his formidable syllabus of errors. What he
was reacting against, in effect, were "two prevailing assumptions about the study of the classic texts in the history of
political thought." The first assumption is akin to that made
by the proponents of the New Criticism in literary studies,
namely, that "the source of a text's intelligibility lies within
itself and its understanding does not require the commentator to consider its context." The second is that "a satisfacto-

ry history can be constructed out of the 'unit-ideas' contained in such texts, or else out of linking such texts in a chain of alleged influences."[53] The second assumption, you should note, he appears to have regarded as a *consequence* of the first, and when he attacked it, it was in an attempt to argue his claim that that first assumption constitutes "a wholly inadequate methodology for the conduct of the history of ideas," one "incapable in principle of considering or even recognizing some of the most crucial problems which arise in any attempt to understand the relations between what a given writer may have *said,* and what he may be said to have meant by saying what he said."[54]

That claim I am not disposed to dispute. But while such a methodology may conceivably have been characteristic of the way in which the history of political thought has been written, I see no grounds at all for equating it with the methodology that Lovejoy himself proposed or that he and his collaborators attempted to apply. The intellectual context of his methodological enterprise was a much broader one and the precision with which he formulated his own stance of a much higher order. Certainly, it would be misleading to represent him as concentrating simply on "studying the form of words involved" and wholly inaccurate to depict his enterprise as constituting "little more than a very misleading fetishism of words."[55] To do so, if I may borrow a remark of John Passmore's, would surely be akin to indulging the pastime of "telling men of straw that they have no brains."[56] (They tend not have any.) The more disappointing, indeed, in the context of a discussion of the meaning of texts and the recovery of authorial intentionality, for Lovejoy wrote about his methodological presuppositions on more than one occasion and at considerable length. To these writings, then—and those who dismiss his approach appear often to have read them with inattention—we must now turn.[57]

III

"One of the safest (and most useful) generalizations re-
sulting from a study of the history of ideas is that every age
tends to exaggerate the scope and finality of its own discov-
eries, or re-discoveries, to be so dazzled with them that it
fails to discern clearly their limitations and forgets aspects of
truth against prior exaggerations of which it has revolted."[58]
These are Lovejoy's words, written in 1940, and appropriately prophetic of the fate of his own methodological views
some thirty or forty years later. Read his essays in historiography with recent discussions in mind and one is in for
something of a surprise. For they resonate in considerable
degree to the same frequency as do the views I have just been
discussing. Not, admittedly, those of structuralist or poststructuralist inspiration. The current vogue of the latter, especially in their deconstructionist guise, he would have seen
above all, I suspect, as a good exemplification of what he
liked to call "metaphysical pathos"—in this case, "the pathos of sheer obscurity, the loveliness of the incomprehensible, which," he said, has "stood many a philosopher in good
stead with his public." "The reader doesn't know exactly
what they [i.e., such philosophers] mean, but they have all
the more on that account an air of sublimity, an agreeable
feeling at once of awe and exaltation comes over him as he
contemplates thoughts of so immeasurable a profundity."[59]
But with the views of Dunn and Skinner Lovejoy would, I
believe, have betrayed a good deal of sympathy.

Certainly, he shared their negative appraisal of much that
has passed as history of ideas,[60] their sensitivity to the ease
with which the historian can impose on the texts he is reading a spurious unity or coherence, harmonizing "the thought
of a reflective writer in such a fashion that what is, historically considered, precisely the most interesting and noteworthy fact about him . . . is wholly concealed."[61] As also

their antipathy toward any treatment of ideas across time that smacks even remotely of what Skinner has called a fetishism of words. Such an insensitivity to usage, he argued (for it is the way in which people actually use words that determines their meaning), can lead us to miss the tissue of ambiguity characteristic of human discourse, the degree to which the same word can be used with a variety of meanings or the same idea signified by a variety of words. It can lead us, in effect, to the sort of "vast terminological confusion" and the "vast amount of bad history" that Lovejoy himself saw as surrounding the topic of Romanticism.[62] Hence the reputation he enjoyed among his own contemporaries as a man possessed of an almost Scotistic capacity for drawing precise distinctions, as the admired discriminator of the multiple meanings of "Romanticism," of the thirteen meanings of pragmatism, of the sixty-six senses in which the word "nature" was used in antiquity.[63] Hence, too, his explicit rejection of the approach to literary studies being promoted in his own day by the advocates of the New Criticism; namely, that "it makes no difference, so far as the aesthetic quality and efficacy of a poem are concerned, who wrote it, or when, or what sort of person he was, or from what motive he wrote it, or even what he meant to convey by it." Good reading, he argued to the contrary, was dependent upon more than a scrutiny of a text's "own literal and explicit content"; it was dependent "upon a knowledge—or an assumption—about what he [the author] was trying to do," something that cannot "always be safely or fully inferred from the obvious content of the work."[64] As a result, he championed a historical, contextual approach to literature. And in literary history, as also in the history of philosophy, where he detected parallel problems, he stressed the danger of too obsessive a preoccupation with masterpieces and the importance, accordingly, of studying the minor writers and thinkers and of grasping the "collective thought" of a given age. Only thus, indeed, is a truly *historical* understanding of the "few great writers" of that age possible.[65]

And so on. It would be possible to list further points of mutual sympathy between the views of Lovejoy and those of his recent critics,[66] but enough has surely been said to make it clear that his approach to the reading of past writings simply does not correspond with that attacked by Skinner—this latter essentially a "New Critical" approach insisting on "the autonomy of the text itself as the sole necessary key to its own meaning."[67] That being so, it seems reasonable to infer that the mode of tracing the morphology of ideas across time which Skinner links with the New Critical approach to texts and dismisses as "wrong in principle" is simply not that which Lovejoy himself either proposed or practiced.

That inference is entirely correct. Three distinct but interrelated motifs dominate Lovejoy's thinking about the history of ideas. The first is that the pursuit of that study must necessarily be interdisciplinary. It is one of the three most general phenomena in the history of ideas, he emphasized in the last of his methodological statements, that "the presence and influence of the same presuppositions or other operative 'ideas'" should be detectable "in very diverse provinces of thought and in different periods." "Ideas", he had said earlier, "are the most migratory things in the world," their study, as a result, is pursued in partial isolation from their contexts under the aegis of at least twelve disciplinary or subdisciplinary enterprises, themselves divided from one another by lines corresponding to "no lines of absolute cleavage in the historical phenomena under investigation."[68] Thus the pressing need to resist the distorting limitations of academic departmentalism by effectively surmounting the barriers that tradition has erected between the disciplines and between those subjects that are divided in terms of nationalities and languages. For the working of a given idea needs, "if its nature and its historic rôle are to be fully understood, to be traced connectedly through all the phases of man's reflective life in which those workings manifest themselves, or through as many of them as the historian's resources permit."[69]

That concluding qualification reflects the second of Lovejoy's motifs, one that dates back to the early days of his career, namely, the need for cooperation or collaboration among specialists in all the pertinent fields, for no one "can be a competent original investigator in many provinces even of history," and anyone interested in the career of ideas "is likely to need assistance, too, from specialists in the non-historical disciplines."[70] The more so if, in accordance with the third of Lovejoy's motifs, one pursues one's study of the history of ideas not by focusing on periods, schools, systems, or -isms, all of which involve "idea-complexes" or compounds, frequently unstable, but by breaking those complexes down, rather in the fashion of an analytical chemist, into their component elements or "unit-ideas." These he regarded as the "persistent dynamic factors" or "recurrent dynamic units" in the history of thought, and he urged as the distinctive program of the history of ideas the tracing of the careers of such unit-ideas across time, as successive thinkers, often in widely differing provinces of intellectual endeavor, brought them into relationship with other unit-ideas, sometimes contradictory, often incompatible, or constructed varying compounds as frequently unstable as they were original.[71] Oddly enough, Lovejoy never proffered a formal definition of a unit-idea, but he described them on more than one occasion, and his combined listings included (among other items, and proceeding from the least to the most definite) types of metaphysical pathos, "implicit or explicit presuppositions," "dialectical motives," "sacred formulas and catchwords," "types of categories," and specific propositions or principles along with their corollaries.[72] This last type of unit-idea he thought "easier to isolate and identify with confidence," and it was on such that he focused his own atten-

tion—most effectively in *The Great Chain of Being*, the jus-
tifiably famous work written when he was almost sixty and
representing the summation of the philosophical as well as
the historical concerns of his entire career.[73]

Beginning with the characteristic observation that "a self-
contradiction does not cease to be meaningless by seeming
sublime,"[74] Lovejoy took as his point of departure the presence within Plato's thought of two conflicting major strains,
each linked with (or grounded in) its own distinct conception
of the divine. The first strain, otherworldly in its emphasis,
he saw as finding its crucial expression in the notion of a
supreme Idea of Ideas which Plato outlined in the *Republic*,
the idea of the Good—eternal, unchanging, truly real, the
self-sufficing perfection, the object of universal desire but
itself in need of nothing apart from it. The second strain,
worldly in its implications, manifests itself in the *Timaeus*,
where Plato, in an attempt to explain why, in addition to the
unchanging idea of the Good, an imperfect world of change or
becoming should exist at all, introduces the figure of the
divine *demiurgos*, a being possessed fully of the attributes of
the idea of the Good (and perhaps in Plato's mind identified
with it). This being's very self-sufficiency and perfection necessitated that it would not be envious of anything not itself,
that it should be "the logical ground as well as the dynamic
source of the existence of a temporal and material and ex-
tremely multiple and variegated universe," peopled by beings
"inherently desirable" despite their finitude and imperfec-
tion.[75] The self-sufficing perfection being by this strange al-
chemy transmuted into a self-transcending fecundity, it
could begrudge existence to nothing that could conceivably
possess it. And in this notion of the necessary realization of
all conceptual possibilities, which he called "the principle of
plenitude," Lovejoy identified the first of the three discrete
unit-ideas that in compound formed the idea-complex
known as the great chain of being.

Of the other two unit-ideas, the first, the principle of continuity, the notion that "if there is between two given natural species a theoretically possible intermediate type, that type must be realized," could have been deduced, Lovejoy noted, from Plato's principle of plenitude. For the presence of gaps in the universe would involve a lack of fullness and imply an inadmissible flaw in the goodness or perfection of the creator.[76] But it was Aristotle, he argued, that actually introduced the principle, as also the third principle, that of "unilinear gradation," itself a combination of his "vague notion of an ontological scale," whereby all individual things were "graded" according to the degree to which they were "infected with [mere] potentiality," with his more concrete notion of zoological and psychological hierarchies, whereby all animals and all organisms were graded hierarchically in accordance with their degree of "perfection" or with the "powers of soul" they possessed.[77]

The idea-complex formed by the linking of these three principles or unit-ideas constituted, Lovejoy said, "the conception of the plan and structure of the world which, through the Middle Ages and down to the late-eighteenth century, many philosophers, most men of science, and indeed, most educated men, were to accept without question—the conception of the universe as a 'Great Chain of Being', composed of an immense, or . . . [even] infinite, number of links ranging in hierarchical order from the meagerest kind of existents, . . . through 'every possible' grade up to the *ens perfectissimum*."[78] Plotinus in the third century first "fully organized" this idea-complex "into a coherent general scheme of things," [79] and on the broad stream of neoplatonism it was borne down through the centuries, finding its clearest expression at the hands of Spinoza and Leibniz and its widest diffusion during the eighteenth century. During that century "writers of all sorts—men of science and philosophers, poets and popular essayists, deists and orthodox divines"—accepted implicitly "the general scheme of ideas connected with it" and "boldly drew from these their latent implications, or apparent implications,"[80] to such a degree, indeed, that the contradictions and difficulties generated thereby led eventually to the breakdown of the notion of a "static and permanently complete Chain of Being," to its temporalizing in evolutionary fashion, and its transformation into "the program of an endless Becoming."[81] That transformation found its culmination during the Romantic era in the thought of Schelling, whose view it was not only that "all genuine possibles are . . . destined to realization, grade after grade, . . . only through a vast, slow unfolding in time," but also that God himself was to be situated in, "or identified with, this Becoming."[82] And with Schelling, Lovejoy drew his account to a close.

That whole account, let it be confessed, reveals a dazzlingly effective combination of careful discrimination, precise argumentation, and enormous erudition. As such, it constitutes an illuminating vindication of the value of Lovejoy's chosen approach to the history of ideas. That approach opens up genuinely historical terrain that is unshadowed, on the one hand, by the fashionable absurdities of some of the structuralists and poststructuralists, but overlooked, on the other, by the somewhat confining rigorisms of Dunn and Skinner. If that approach unquestionably leaves out of account much that appears to belong to intellectual history, Lovejoy was fully aware of the fact and acknowledged that *his* history of ideas would necessarily depend greatly on "the prior labors" of "the other branches of the history of thought."[83] If it is indeed open to criticism, it is so not on the grounds that Skinner adduces, for it betrays no disposition to slight the meanings intended by the authors of the texts with which it deals or to ignore the contextual studies necessary if those meanings are to be identified with any sort of precision. There is a sense, in fact, in which its particular program enriches that context and eases that task of identification, for it is particularly sensitive to the impact of the written word, cognizant of the degree to which an author may be responding to questions posed by thinkers predating him even by centuries, or may be nudged along his path by the pressure, the logical promptings, the "particular go" (Lovejoy's phrase)[84] of an idea he has appropriated. It is a program mindful of the extent, therefore, to which the community in the context of which that author does his thinking includes not only the living, but also the dead.[85] If it is to be criticized at all, the neuralgic point of Lovejoy's approach appears to be situated in the degree to which, misled by the analogy he himself had drawn from analytical chemistry, he treated his unit-ideas as if they were things, unchanging atomic particles, incapable themselves of possessing a history, that history belonging instead to the progress of their relationships with other ideas, their entering into or breaking away from other idea-complexes.[86] But even if one were to concede the validity of that criticism, it is noteworthy that those who make it agree that in his actual historical practice, if not in his programmatic methodological statements, Lovejoy either focused his attention on idea-complexes such as the great chain of being, which certainly do change across time, or tended to treat his unit-ideas less as elements than as dynamic forces—that is, as idea-complexes.[87]

This last point is noteworthy on other grounds, too. Speaking of the history of political thought, Pocock has argued that "good work done in a context of methodological confusion is in a sense done by chance, or by some coincidence of *virtù* and *fortuna*; it is done despite the available methods, and lacks the critical autonomy which comes only when the method is operating positively to produce the work."[88] About that, however, I am not so sure. Those of us who are historians have often been somewhat derisive about the inadequacy of philosophic attempts to construe the nature and presuppositions of historical inquiry and to identify the epistemological status of historical propositions.[89] We ourselves, however, rarely succeed in doing much better. Even when we import philosophical notions in an attempt to analyze our own methodological assumptions and procedures (perhaps especially then), a hardening of the intellectual arteries seems characteristically to occur. The prose becomes labored, the vital passages become constricted, the head aches, and a drowsy numbness strains the sense. The very density, intricacy, and richness of our own historical tactic persistently escapes, it seems, the conceptual net in which we struggle so persistently to confine it. This is true of Dunn, of Pocock, of Skinner—all of them highly skilled historians, the importance of whose historical contributions no one, I assume, would want to question. And it was true also, as we have seen, of Lovejoy himself, whose own contributions as an historian can certainly sustain comparison with theirs.

If, then, I propose to strike off on a line of march that will take me away from the highroad constituted by the history of the great chain of being and across rough and less well-mapped terrain, in so doing I have had the temerity to propose to myself not one but two goals. The first is to add a worthwhile footnote to Lovejoy, or, put somewhat less self-effacingly, to chart from the twelfth to the seventeenth centuries the history of a theme—unit-idea, idea-complex, call it what you will—that during those centuries constituted the chief rival, as pivot of a coherent scheme of things entire, to the notion of the great chain of being itself. The second is, by so doing, to attempt a vindication of the validity, efficacy, and fruitfulness of Lovejoy's improperly maligned approach to the history of ideas. For I believe that this can best be done, if I may borrow words that Lucien Febvre wrote in introducing the first issue of the *Annales*, "not by means of articles about method, not by means of theoretical disquisitions, but by means of examples, by means of achieved results."[90]

Chapter 2

ST. JEROME AND THE SAD
CASE OF THE FALLEN VIRGIN

> I will speak boldly; although God can do all things,
> he cannot raise up a virgin after she has fallen.
> —St. Jerome

I

Historians have ceased long since to lay much stress on the year A.D. 476, when Odovacar, leader of an invading barbarian confederacy, took over Italy and deposed the youth who has gone down in history as the last of the Roman emperors of the West. Those anxious, indeed, to pinpoint a moment of symbolic discontinuity in the transition from the ancient to the medieval worlds might do better to focus on the year 410, when, as St. Jerome laments, Rome, "the city which had taken the whole world, was itself taken,"[1] sacked by the invading Goths. The city had remained inviolate for almost 800 years—since, in effect, that mythic moment when, as Livy assures us, only the warning given by the sacred geese (*clangore eorum alarumque crepitu*) had saved the capitol itself from shameful seizure by the Gauls²—and, or so the reaction of Jerome and Augustine, the two greatest of the Latin fathers of the church, suggest, the imaginative impact of the Gothic attack on the people of the day was enormous. In Jerome, living out his last years in the monastery at Bethlehem, it stimulated a deep and debilitating personal grief.³ Augustine, closer to Rome but safe at least for the time being in North Africa, it prompted to write *De civitate dei.* And it prompted him to address in the first book of that great work a topic dear to both of them: virginity.

Augustine's message on that occasion was one of consolation to the helpless victims of rape at Rome.⁴ But it was Jerome's earlier message to Rome, his famous letter to Eustochium lauding the grandeur of virginity,⁵ that was destined, if I may sidle up now to the matter at hand, to inaugurate a medieval debate of no little consequence. Not, admittedly, in any way that Jerome could have intended. And not for some time. But then, though intellectuals often but oddly overlook the fact, it is well to be reminded of how large a part books play in their lives, of how, through books, their society is peopled with the dead, of how so often they hear or make the dead to speak in new and frequently vibrant ways.

II

The time, then: well over six centuries later, probably the year 1067. The place: the great abbey of Monte Cassino in southern Italy. At a table two men are deep in conversation. The one: Desiderius, rector of the monastery; the other: Peter Damiani, sometime bishop, church reformer, saint, and in his day no less renowned an ascetic than Jerome had been. In the middle of the conversation, some of the words of Jerome to Eustochium are quoted. Remarking with due humility that one has to pay attention not simply to who it is that is speaking but to what he is actually saying, Damiani confesses that he has never been able to accept that particular claim of Jerome's. Desiderius disagrees. A long and prolix argument ensues. The subsequent outcome: a celebrated disputation by Damiani.[6]

In the passage in question, Jerome had written as follows: "I will speak boldly: although God can do all things, he cannot raise up a virgin after she has fallen" (*cum omnia Deus possit, suscitare virginem non potest post ruinam*).[7] His point in so writing appears to have been to underline the enormity of the loss involved. For Damiani, however, the issue is a different one. He writes, he says, not "in order to disparage the blessed Jerome, who spoke with religious devotion, but to confute by the invincible reasoning of the faith those who made of his words an occasion for imputing a lack of power to God."[8] Hence *his* topic: the divine omnipotence, which he addresses with great vigor and ill-concealed contempt for the wiles of those dialecticians who raised so "superstitious," so "superfluous," so "cunning" a question (*superstitiosa quaestio, supervacua quaestio, versuta quaestio*).[9] "Out of nothing, nothing comes," say the philosophers, but God, who has no need of any creature and is nudged by no necessity to create, out of that nothing into existence draws this natural world of ours, establishing its order, imposing upon it its customary laws. Incapable in his omnipotence and in his eternal present of suffering any diminution or alteration of his creative power, that natural order he could well replace, those laws at any moment change. This, "to confound the arguments of the philosophers" and "to overthrow the . . . syllogisms of the dialecticians," he has proved again and again, as he did when in his hand he held unscathed the three youths cast into Nebuchadnezzar's fiery furnace. How, then, dare we doubt that God can restore the virginity of a fallen woman? And how, if the wily dialecticians transpose that question into a more abstract and principled key, how can we deny that God can undo the past—that is, so act that an actual historical event should not have occurred?[10] And if the profane purveyors of a merely human reason should complain that such would contravene the law of noncontradiction, so be it. So much the worse, it would seem, for that principle.[11]

These are strong words, and they are rich in implications that we must eventually address. For the moment, however, let me content myself with noting that with those words Damiani, whose name Lovejoy never mentions, brings us back, willy-nilly, to the matter of the great chain of being. In discussing the genesis of that notion, you may recall, Lovejoy was at pains to stress that as a complex idea it embraced in fact "Two-Gods-in-One." In the first place, God as goodness itself, overflowing into creation like a mountain lake giving birth to a stream, moved by the inherent generosity and very necessity of his nature to bring into being everything even remotely conceivable, and therefore, as must be conceded once the implications of this principle of plenitude are fully grasped, necessitated to produce the best of all possible worlds. In the second place, God as the good, of whose very essence it is to be self-sufficient perfection, lacking, therefore, in his nature, any reason or desire "to bring a universe of imperfect beings into existence," with the result that the creative act must "be conceived to be entirely groundless and arbitrary in itself, and therefore in its inclusions and exclusions." Complex enough, but as Lovejoy duly noted in discussing the subsequent development of the notion, the plot thickened when, during the early Christian era, there was in the third place added to those two previous Gods yet another—the God of Abraham, Isaac, and Jacob, the biblical God of might and power, "the Jewish conception of a temporal Creator and busy interposing Power making for righteousness through the hurly-burly of history."[12]

As that fusion of three Gods into one being was in his view "perhaps the most extraordinary triumph of self-contradiction, among many such triumphs in the history of human thought,"[13] it is not surprising that Lovejoy should have stressed the harshness of the dilemmas confronting orthodox medieval thinkers eager nonetheless to respond to the full notion of the divine handed down to them in all its richness. The fate of Peter Abelard, writing only about half a century after Damiani, is, he says, a case in point. In his *Introduction to Theology*, it was to the ambivalent promptings of Plato's *Timaeus* that Abelard responded most urgently, and then with self-consciously uneasy faithfulness to the first of Plato's Gods. Setting out from "the principles of sufficient reason and of plenitude, as these were implicit in the accepted meaning of the doctrine of the goodness of deity, . . . Abelard saw clearly that these premises led to a necessitarian optimism." The world, therefore, has to be "the best possible world." In it "all genuine possibility must be actualized." And that is to say that "none of its characteristics or components can be contingent, but all things must have been precisely what they are."[14]

Although Abelard does not fail to quote in support of his position Jerome's deliverance on the case of the fallen virgin,[15] it was clearly not a position that any Christian who wished to respond faithfully to the biblical vision of a God of freedom, power, and might could consistently maintain. On this point, some of his followers may have had the temerity to echo his opinion, but it was, in fact, one of the grounds for Abelard's condemnation in 1140. Accordingly, the most influential theologians of the latter part of the century—notably Hugh of St. Victor and Peter Lombard—sought to distance themselves from him and to scramble back onto safer doctrinal ground.[16] So, too, Thomas Aquinas a century later. Maneuver adroitly, however, though he might, deploying a brave platoon of scholastic distinctions marshaled to render compatible the contradictory and harmonious the dissonant, in Lovejoy's view at least he was no more successful in evad-

ing outright contradiction on this point than was Leibniz,
several centuries later, in distinguishing his own necessitarianism from that of Abelard.[17]

Leibniz's failure was hardly surprising, because what
Abelard had done was to draw from "Plato's premise the
most characteristic of Spinoza's conclusions," and that, according to Lovejoy, was the same as saying that he had
"drawn from that premise its true consequence."[18] For it was
those who wanted desperately to respond to the divine amal-
gam in all its contradictory richness that were threatened
with theological schizophrenia, and not those who, like Spinoza in the seventeenth century or Giordano Bruno in the
sixteenth, were willing to place their full emphasis on the
first of Plato's Gods—God, you will recall, as goodness itself,
logically necessitated by the generosity and perfection of his
own being not only to produce a world, but also to produce
the best and most complete of conceivable worlds. And not,
Lovejoy adds, "those extreme anti-rationalists, represented
in the later Middle Ages by the Scotists, William of Ockham,
and others," who, placing their stress on the biblical notion
of God as mighty will and irresistible power, "held the arbitrary and inscrutable will of the deity to be the sole ground"
not only of the existence of the world but also "of all distinctions of value" in that world.[19]

On this last point Lovejoy was in the main correct. But,
while signaling an appropriate measure of deference, I should
like now to append two qualifications to the claim he was
making. First, that while on this matter of the relationship of
God to the world the late-medieval voluntarists were indeed
less troubled souls than most of their earlier medieval predecessors, they owed that privilege in some measure to the
worried dialectical labors of some of those earlier scholastics.
Second, that while some issues were (or had become) easier
for these later-medieval thinkers, others, given the intellectual upheaval occasioned during the late twelfth and thir-

teenth centuries by the great influx of Aristotelian and Arab philosophical and scientific writings, others had become harder. They were, therefore, less untroubled souls than Lovejoy imagined. To these two qualifications we must now address ourselves.

III

In *The Great Chain of Being* Lovejoy's concern is primarily with the relation between God and the world in the order of creation. When he discusses such medieval thinkers as Abelard, Peter Lombard, Thomas Aquinas, that is to say, he is concerned with God's creative act and the degree to which that act is so determined by the divine being, its goodness and rationality, that God has to act as he does, it being impossible for him either to do otherwise or to do better. Now it is important to realize that the thinkers with whom Lovejoy is dealing raised this issue not in isolation, but in the context of a discussion of the divine attributes in general and the divine power in particular. In so doing, and following cues given to them by Augustine,[20] they struggled first to clarify the relationship between God's power and his other attributes, notably his will. All were agreed that if you take God's willing to mean that which by his providence he ordains to come about, God can certainly do whatever he wills. The matter in dispute was whether God's attribute of omnipotence requires us to believe that he has the power to do otherwise or better than he has in fact willed to do. It was to this question that Abelard rendered his uneasy denial, thereby subjecting himself to the criticisms of such as Hugh of St. Victor and Peter Lombard, who, although they were convinced he was wrong, were forced to struggle all the harder to solve the puzzle of how, then, God's power was to be related to those other attributes of will, reason, and goodness.

The ultimate outcome of such labors was, appropriately enough, the emergence of a scholastic distinction concerning the divine power which, though it did not enjoy so prolonged a history as did the notion of the great chain of being, and never attained to the sort of ubiquity enjoyed by the latter in the eighteenth century, deserves much closer and wider attention than it has yet received from historians. In its late-medieval and early-modern form, at least, that distinction constituted nothing less than the pivot on which turned a vision of the nature of the universe rivaling in its logical force and imaginative appeal the vision associated with the notion of the great chain of being. Although some harbingers of its formation occurred during the twelfth century, it was not until the early years of the thirteenth that the distinction in question appears finally to have crystallized.[21] Despite his searching scrutiny of the divine attributes, the tendency of St. Anselm's theologizing lay in a different direction,[22] and notwithstanding suggestions to the contrary, the distinction is not to be found in Hugh of St. Victor. If Albertus Magnus, Aquinas' teacher, implies that by his own day its use had become customary, his own formulation (dating to about 1260) remains nonetheless one of the earliest ones known to us. Quite brief, it is set in the context of a discussion that carefully relates God's omnipotence not only to his will but to such other attributes as his wisdom and justice, and we are cautioned that nothing is to be attributed to God's power that would detract from his goodness or truth. That being understood, he introduces a distinction between God's "absolute" and "ordained" powers (*potentia dei absoluta et ordinata*). If the divine power is taken absolutely, then God is "an ocean of infinite power" and "there is nothing that he cannot do." If taken as ordained, however, that power must be understood as being disposed in accord with his providence and goodness.[23] Or, as Aquinas was to put it, taking over the distinction from his master,

> what is attributed to [his] power considered in itself, God is
> said to be able to do by his absolute power. . . . As for what is
> attributed to his power as carrying out the command of his
> just will, he is said to be able to do by his ordained power. . . .
> Accordingly, it should be said that by his absolute power
> God can do things other than those he foresaw that he would
> do and preordained so to do. Nevertheless nothing can come
> to be that he has not foreseen and pre-ordained; for his doing
> falls under his foreknowing and pre-ordaining, not the power
> of his doing, for that is his nature, not his choice.[24]

Succinctly put, no doubt, perhaps too much so, and it is
easy enough to miss or to mistake the point he is making.
What he is in the process of doing when he introduces the
distinction in the *Summa theologiae* is discussing the divine
omnipotence in general and such pertinent questions in particular as "Can God make what had been not to have been?"
"Can God do what he does not do?" "Could God make better
things than he does?"[25] Good questions all. Certainly ones
familiar already to us, and Aquinas does not fail to refer both
to Jerome's enduringly popular sentiments on the sad case of
the fallen virgin or to the related opinion for which Abelard
had been condemned.[26] But writing, as he did, in the wake of
the great reception of Aristotelian philosophy which arrived
intertwined with the views of such Muslim philosophers as
Ibn Sina and Ibn Rushd (Avicenna and Averroës), he was
concerned to steer clear not only of Abelard's position but
also of the much greater threat posed by the more thoroughgoing philosophic determinism of those philosophers
who, he tells us, argued that "from God's workings there
cannot proceed effects or an arrangement of effects other
than those presently prevailing."[27] At the same time, he had
to be careful to avoid the opposed excesses of those Muslim
theologians who, in their attempts to vindicate against the
neoplatonists and Aristotelians of their own day the divine
freedom and omnipotence, he understood so to have outDa-

mianied Damiani as to have inadvertently belittled God's
goodness by denying any efficacy at all to second causes.[28]

As a result, the appeal of the distinction between the absolute and ordained powers of God lay for him in the fact that it
was a valuable dialectical tool easing the way to a reinforcement of his earlier claim that in creation "God's will," which
itself knows no cause, "is the cause of things."[29] This he did
by adding now the further claim that "the present course of
things," which reflects God's ordained power and represents
but one possible expression of the divine wisdom, goodness,
and justice, "does not proceed from his will by such necessity
that other arrangements [speaking now of his absolute power]
could not have been made."[30] But the stress lies, you should
note, on the "could." As Alexander of Hales had put it even
before Albertus Magnus wrote, "the absolute power pertains
to those things concerning which there is no divine preordina-
tion; the ordained power . . . to those things which have been
preordained or disposed by God."[31] The absolute power refers
to God's ability to do many things that he does not choose to
do. It refers, that is,

> to the total possibilities *initially* open to God, some of
> which were realized by creating the established order; the
> unrealized possibilities are now only hypothetically possi-
> ble. Viewed another way, the *potentia absoluta* is God's
> power considered absolutely, . . . without taking into ac-
> count the order established by God. *Potentia ordinata*, on
> the other hand, is the total ordained will of God, the com-
> plete plan of God for his creation.[32]

The stress, therefore, lies on the realm of the ordained power,
which evokes the stable, concrete arrangements that the
good God, who never acts in a disorderly or arbitrary fashion,
has preordained in his creation, has actually chosen to effect,
and that we humans can, therefore, safely rely upon. At the
same time, the absolute power remains, as it were, on dialec-

tical standby, a matter of abstract possibility periodically evoked to underline the contingency of creation, the world's dependence, that is, on the untrammeled decision of the divine will, the fact that it does not have either to be what it is or even to be at all.

By the fourteenth century this distinction had already become something of a cliché, and its availability in the dialectical arsenal clearly made their philosophical and theological endeavors easier for those later-medieval thinkers whom Lovejoy called "extreme anti-rationalists." Certainly, though there are hesitations in some of his formulations, the distinction was given a warm welcome by William of Ockham, who is now thought to have understood it in much the same way as did Aquinas.[33] It enjoyed a continuing vogue among theologians and philosophers throughout the fourteenth and fifteenth centuries, survived during the sixteenth the ambivalent strictures of Luther[34] and the general ideological turbulence of the Reformation era, and was still being evoked in the early seventeenth century by such Catholic thinkers as Francisco Suárez and by such Protestants as the great Puritan divine William Ames. This last piece of information is particularly important because Ames's classic textbook, the *Medulla theologica*, first published in 1623 in Amsterdam, was widely read in Holland, England, and New England, the Latin edition going through twelve printings, a Dutch translation appearing in 1656, and three printings of an English translation—*The Marrow of Sacred Divinity*—appearing between 1638 and 1643, one of them "by order from the Honorable the House of Commons."[35] We should not be surprised then, if, while leafing through the collected sermons of the Reverend Samuel Willard, we find in *Sermon XXII* (published in Boston in 1726), the following statement:

> Divines do from Scripture observe a twofold Power ascribed to God, viz. 1. An unlimited and absolute Power, by virtue of which he can do all possible things, even such things as he

never actually doth: of this Power it is that we read *Matth.
3:9*—*God is able of these stones to raise up children unto
Abraham.* 2. An ordinate Power, which is not a Power different from the former, but the former considered, as God hath
pleased to set limits or bounds to it by the Decree, with
respect to his exerting of it in his works of Efficiency. It is
certain that he hath by an Eternal purpose, determined in
himself whatsoever shall be done in time, and this did un-
alterably fix the limits between things merely possible, and
things future.[36]

IV

I mentioned earlier the presence of hesitations in some of
Ockham's formulations of this extraordinarily durable distinction. While in general his usage appears to be more or less
aligned with that of Aquinas,[37] from time to time he slips
into an identification of the realm of the ordained power with
what God can be said to do "in accordance with the laws
ordained or instituted" by him, or "in accordance with the
common course of nature," or, introducing a historical di-
mension and focusing attention on the new dispensation introduced by Christ as opposed to the Old Law, "in accordance with the law now instituted." And he slips into
illustrating the distinction by adducing the example of the
pope, who, in absolute terms, can do things that he cannot do
"in accord with the law he himself has decreed."[38] I say
"slips" into employing such phrases and examples because
what they inevitably suggest, even though Ockham possibly
did not so intend, is that God's absolute power, far from
referring solely to the possibilities initially open to God, is a
presently active power working, like the dispensing power of
a monarch, to contravene the laws he has himself established. And that brings me to my second point—that while
by Ockham's lifetime some things had become easier for

philosophers and theologians addressing the question of God's relationship to the universe, others had become harder.

It seems safe to speculate that the only problem that Peter Damiani, two and a half centuries earlier, would have had with Ockham's uneasy formulations would have been to find them insufficiently forthright and explicit. Damiani's God, after all, knows no yesterday, today, or tomorrow, but only a perpetual now. The mighty power he exercised in creating the world remains unchanged and unchained. That same power he can still assuredly exercise within what is to us (but not to him) time.[39] And he can do so in a manner subversive even of past history. For he is the sovereign lord, not merely of nature, but even, it seems, of logic.

The subsequent flowering of scholastic philosophy, of course, and the heightened rationalism that went with it, had by Ockham's day long since rendered such unqualified views unfashionable. But it is now time to insist that the very degree of success attained by that rationalism had come to generate the difficulties to which Ockham's uneasy formulations obliquely witness. *The* great intellectual event of the years separating Ockham from Damiani was the recovery of the entire corpus of Aristotle's writings.[40] These works arrived in Western Europe interwoven confusingly with the paraphrases and commentaries of Avicenna and Al-Fārābī (and later of Averroës, too), forcing upon the attention of the scholastic philosophers and theologians an understanding of the divine and its relationship with the natural world which was much harder to reconcile with the biblical vision than the Platonic and neoplatonic viewpoint, which, as we have seen, was capable of generating its own problems. Indeed, under the form in which they frequently encountered it (with the original pattern of Aristotle's thinking overlaid by motifs of neoplatonic and Arab provenance), it was an understanding that appeared to involve an insistence not only on the necessity of the world but also on its eternity, and a denial not only of the providence of God but also of the free will of man and of any form of individual immortality.

To such a viewpoint the ecclesiastical authorities at Paris, the intellectual capital of Christendom, could well respond with a nervous flurry of condemnations. But for the philosophers and theologians of Paris any firm decision to turn their backs on Aristotle's metaphysics and natural philosophy would have been a decision also to turn their backs on the most advanced intellectual trends of their day. Understandably, they opted instead for the difficult alternative of trying to make him acceptable by penetrating beyond the Aristotle of the Arab commentators to the authentic teachings of the philosopher himself and, further, by understanding those teachings from a resolutely Christian perspective. Much of Aquinas' massive intellectual effort was devoted to that end. In that attempt he and those predecessors whose goals he shared both succeeded and failed. Succeeded, in that by 1256 (when he became a master of theology at Paris) all the known writings of Aristotle had been included in the university curriculum—by any estimate an extraordinary turn-around. Failed, in that only three years after Aquinas' death in 1274 Etienne Tempier, bishop of Paris and himself a theologian, formally condemned as contrary to the Christian faith a host of philosophical propositions, including some that could be attributed to Aquinas.

In so decreeing, Tempier acted neither idiosyncratically nor in isolation. Behind his condemnations lay the advice of a commission of sixteen theologians, including Henry of Ghent. Behind them, too, lay the fear, widespread earlier among the more orthodox Muslim thinkers[41] and strongly felt by many of the scholastic theologians of his own day, that the thoroughgoing rationalism of Aristotle and of the less critical of his Muslim and Christian followers endangered the fundamental belief in the freedom and omnipotence of God which was common to both religions. The scenario was certainly different from what it had been in Abelard's case. But not even the skilled philosophical and theological seamanship of Aquinas had enabled him quite to steer clear of the dangerous waters in which Abelard had come to grief. If Lovejoy thought that on this matter Aquinas had succeeded in running afoul of a shoal of contradictions, so, too, it seems, did some of the most influential of Aquinas' contemporaries.

The outcome? The quickening of a theological reaction already under way which was eventually to call into question that whole participatory metaphysic of essences and internal relations upon which the notion of the great chain of being depended and to vindicate the freedom and omnipotence of God at the price of diminishing the ultimate intelligibility of the world. Subsequent theologians and philosophers had to do their thinking in the harsh light of this coercive clarification, and it is not surprising that many of them tended to take the divine freedom and omnipotence as their fundamental principles, asserting in their analyses of the divine psychology the primacy of will over reason (a reversal of Aquinas' priorities) and emphasizing in their discussions of the order of the created world less any sort of participation in a luminous divine reason than utter dependence on an inscrutable divine will.[42]

The distinction between the absolute and ordained powers of God being a piece of weaponry already deployed along this particular firing line, it is understandable that it underwent a certain amount of modification. By the turn of the century this is evident in thinkers of as different philosophical tendency as Aegidius Romanus, a man of quasi-Thomistic sympathies, and Duns Scotus, founder of the philosophical tradition that, during the remainder of the Middle Ages, rivaled the Thomist in its strength and appeal.

For Aegidius, while God (like the pope) possesses a "regulated" power whereby he governs things in accordance with "the common laws" he himself has put into nature, permitting fire to burn, water to moisten, and so on, he possesses also an absolute power or plenitude of power whereby he can set aside the operation of such secondary causes and act "apart from [*praeter*] the common course of nature." As, indeed, he did when he miraculously delivered Mishach, Shadrach, and Abednego from Nebuchadnezzar's fiery furnace.[43] Similarly Scotus, though perhaps not quite so bluntly, distinguished (by analogy not only with kings but with any free agent within whose power the law falls) between the ordained power whereby God acts *de jure*, in accordance with the rightful law he has himself established, and the absolute power whereby *de facto* he can act apart from or against that law. It was understood, moreover, that there is nothing "inordinate" or disorderly about such an action, for the very rectitude of the law derives from God's will, and it is within his power to decree another law in accordance with which his *de facto* action would become, in effect, *de jure*.[44]

If the surfacing of such formulations at the beginning of the fourteenth century may well explain the hesitations evident in Ockham's use of the distinction, such was their currency three-quarters of a century later that Pierre d'Ailly, one of the leading scholastics and churchmen of his day, could insist that they conveyed a "more proper" (*magis proprius*) understanding of the ordained power than did the older usage that limited God *de potentia ordinata* to being able to do "only those things which he himself ordained that he would do."[45] Hence, in his own very frequent usage of the distinction d'Ailly does not hesitate to illustrate the operation of God's absolute power by invoking the analogy of the king's absolute power,[46] and he is prone to speak of God as acting "naturally" when he acts in accordance with his ordained power, and as acting "supernaturally or miraculously" when he acts by his absolute power, breaching thereby "the common law" or "common course of nature."[47]

Two centuries later d'Ailly's "more proper" had matured
into Suárez' "more usual" (*magis usitatus*). And, as if to underline the fact that the contrast he had in mind was one
between, on the one hand, God's power taken without qualification, apart from any "determination of his will and without any respect to the nature of things or other causes," and,
on the other, God's power as it operated "in accord with the
common laws and causes which he has established in the
universe"—as if to underline that fact, the phrase Suárez
sometimes used in contrast with *potentia absoluta* was not
potentia ordinata but *potentia ordinaria*, thereby suggesting
that we should think of the absolute power less as a matter of
abstract or hypothetical possibility than as an extraordinary
power of miraculous interposition.[48]

He was not alone in so doing. Martin Luther, who had
earlier dismissed the distinction as a piece of scholastic so-
phistry, later used it in exactly the same way, employing
interchangeably the terms "absolute" and "extraordinary,"
on the one hand, and "ordained" and "ordinary," on the
other, treating the former as God's miraculous power, the
power that deprived the flames of their natural effect and
delivered the three youths from Nebuchadnezzar's fiery furnace.[49] Many another, Catholic as well as Protestant, had
drifted in the same direction,[50] but, limiting myself to one
example, let me refer to the lectures on the first book of Peter
Lombard's *Sentences* which Dr. Johann Eck, Luther's old op-
ponent, delivered in 1542. I pick them not because they were
influential (they were published for the first time only in
1976), still less because they were in any way distinguished.
Rather because they can be presumed to reflect all too
faithfully the overworked scholastic clichés of the day. And,
sure enough, in commenting on the forty-second, forty-third,
and forty-fourth distinctions, where Lombard had wrestled
with those questions concerning the divine power which had
exercised Damiani and brought Abelard to grief (whether
God could undo the past, whether he could have made things

other than he had or a world better than he did)—in discussing those venerable questions, Eck evoked once more
Jerome's opinion on the sad case of the fallen virgin and
flourished the divine delivery of Mishach, Shadrach, and
Abednego from the flames. This last, of course, to illustrate
an actual historical exercise by God of his absolute power,
when he chose to act apart from "the common law," "common course," or "common rule which he put into things,"
which, of his ordained power, he normally observes.[51]

Eck still used the expression *potentia ordinata*, and it may
have evoked for him uneasy echoes of the older usage, for he
hastened to insist that God in exercising his absolute power
does not act in a disorderly fashion (*inordinate*). And it is the
divine will, of course, that makes something to be just. But in
order to avoid confusion, he mused, perhaps it would be better
to think also in terms of God's ordination of things as being
special as well as general. Thus it is in accord with God's
"general ordained power" that fire should burn and consume
what it touches. But when by the absolute power the three
youths were not consumed by the flames of Nebuchadnezzar's
furnace, that result can be said to have come about by God's
"special ordained power" because "God had foreseen it from
all eternity."[52]

It was left, then, for some of the great Puritan divines of the
seventeenth century (in this, at least, true successors to the
medieval scholastics) to pursue the logic of the differing
usages to which both d'Ailly and Suárez had drawn attention
and to bring a final clarity to the issue by proposing the
adoption of distinct terminologies for them. Thus, in *The
Marrow of Sacred Divinity*, William Ames, in distinguishing
between the absolute and ordained or actual powers of God,
ascribes to that distinction, and with admirable concision, the
older meaning favored by Aquinas. The "absolute power," he
says, "is that by which God is able to do all things possible
though they may never be done." "The ordained power," on
the other hand, "is that by which he not only can do what he

wills but does actually do what he wills."53 At the same time, however, Ames does not forget the newer meaning, which, according to Suárez, had by his lifetime become more common among the scholastics. But he renders it by referring to "the ordinary and usual" or "extraordinary and unusual" providence of God, the former consisting in "God's observance of that order in things which was appointed from the beginning" and which "in natural things is the law of nature common to all things," the latter consisting in "God's provision for things beyond the usual and appointed order." And, he adds, "whatever is [so] effected is, by metonymy of the effect, called a miracle."54

Not all of the Puritan divines, either in England or in New England, were as clearheaded on this score as was Ames. In their writings, the focus tends to be, as with Increase Mather and Thomas Shepherd, on the distinction between the ordinary and extraordinary providence of God.55 But, in mid-century, both distinctions were given their due place in John Norton's *Orthodox Evangelist*, and, at the beginning of the eighteenth century, in Samuel Willard's *Compleat Body of Divinity*.56 It was not customary for such men to cite the Catholic Church Fathers, and virginity was not for them a preferred vocation. But if St. Jerome's deliverance on the case of the fallen virgin appears now to have receded definitively into history, the startling events in Nebuchadnezzar's fiery furnace had not, and they were repeatedly invoked to illustrate the wondrous workings of God's extraordinary providence.57

V

So much, then, for the theological history of the distinction between the absolute and ordained powers of God. It was a remarkable history if for no other reason than the extraordinary durability of the distinction, which, more or less intact,

survived, after all, two truly major ideological upheavals—
that occasioned by the reception of Aristotle and its subsequent repercussions, and that occasioned by the Protestant
Reformation. It remains, however, to determine what significance can properly be attached to that remarkable history.

In the course of two of his lengthier discussions of the
distinction, William of Ockham takes note, rather ruefully it
may be, of the confusion surrounding the distinction and
warns of the ease with which anyone who "has not been
excellently instructed in logic and theology" can fall into
error on the matter.[58] The marked disagreement among modern commentators over its meaning and significance witness-
es powerfully to the pertinence of that warning. Our failure
until very recently to realize that the distinction underwent
the mutation I have attempted to describe is in part responsible for this disagreement.[59] More to the point, however, is
the failure of so many commentators to grasp the extent to
which Scotus, Ockham, the latter's nominalist followers,
and so many other late-medieval thinkers were responding in
their use of the distinction to promptings essentially conservative in nature and biblical in provenance. Thus it has not
been at all uncommon—and especially among those concerned with the theology of grace and the questions that were
to be central to the Reformation era—to regard its widespread deployment in the later Middle Ages as a symptom of
the incipient collapse of the whole scholastic endeavor to
harmonize reason and revelation. Ockham in particular and
the nominalists in general have been represented as wielding
the distinction with skeptical, even mischievous intent, despite reassurances to the contrary collapsing the ordained
into the absolute power, introducing thereby all sorts of fan-
tasies into theology, transforming "the entire foundation
of . . . [God's] ordained law" into the most fleeting of con-
tingencies ever liable to be dispensed with," "throwing all
certainty, morality, and indeed probability into the melting

pot," creating a mere as-if theology prone to marginalizing the divine assurances revealed to us in the Scriptures and handed down to us by tradition, calling into question even, under the looming shadow of the divine omnipotence, the very necessity of church, priesthood, and sacraments.[60]

The fact that we now know the distinction not merely to have been invoked in philosophical and theological treatises intended for a rather rarefied intellectual readership but to have made its presence felt also in discussions of mysticism and in the writings of late-medieval and early-modern lawyers,[61] to have cropped up in the sermons of such establishment figures as Pierre d'Ailly at the turn of the fourteenth and fifteenth centuries or in those of the preachers at the papal court at the turn of the fifteenth and sixteenth centuries, to have surfaced later on in the polemics of a traditionalist such as Sir Thomas More, the catechetical manuals or sermons of such stern Puritans as Dudley Fenner, William Ames, and Samuel Willard[62]—this fact alone suggests the improbability of such interpretations and lends color to the sincerity of Ockham's claim that this "common distinction of the theologians," when "sensibly understood, is in harmony with the orthodox faith."[63]

Ockham makes that claim, moreover, in the context of an attack on Pope John XXII for having allegedly implied in one of his sermons that everything comes about by necessity and nothing in a manner completely contingent. And if that should serve to remind us of the degree to which the invocation of the absolute power had consistently been motivated by the wish to vindicate the Old Testament vision of Yahweh as a personal God of power and might against the threat of philosophic determinism, the recent trend of scholarly interpretation has been such as to suggest that the affiliated discrimination of a divine ordained power is likewise a response to another fundamental biblical theme—that of God's promise and covenant.[64]

A considerable significance attaches to this fact. The only force, after all, capable of binding omnipotence without thereby denying it is the omnipotent will itself. Whereas God, therefore, cannot be said to be constrained by the natural order of things or bound by the canons of any merely human reason or justice, he is certainly capable by his own decision of binding himself to follow a stable pattern in dealing with his creation in general and with man in particular. If God has freely chosen the established order, he *has* so chosen, and while he can dispense with or act apart from the laws he has decreed, he has nonetheless bound himself by his promise and will remain faithful to the covenant that, of his kindness and mercy, he has instituted with man.

This covenantal theme is particularly evident in the way in which the nominalist theologians of the later Middle Ages deployed the distinction between the two powers in order to protect the freedom and omnipotence of God without being led thereby to assert a doctrine of predestination *ante praevisa merita*—one, that is, whereby God bases his dread decision not on any foreknowledge of the degree of moral responsibility with which men contrive to lead their lives, but on a secret and inscrutable justice that transcends the categories of any merely human equity. By his absolute power, of course, God *can* justify men by grace alone and predestine them to eternal happiness regardless of their deeds. He is no man's debtor; of themselves, and without the conjunction of grace, human actions, however worthy, are incapable of meriting salvation. Of his ineffable mercy and by his ordained power, however, God has chosen to accept men as partners in the work of their salvation. He has done so in such a fashion that if, of their natural powers, they freely do the best they can (*faciunt quod in se est*), he will confer upon them that habit of sanctifying grace by which alone, in the dispensation now established, acts that are morally good can be transformed into acts that merit an eternal

reward. Accordingly, while these thinkers can still speak of
God's predestination of the elect, it is very much a pre-
destination *post praevisa merita,* one grounded, that is, in
God's foreknowledge of man's meritorious deeds.[65]

Similarly the later-medieval use of the distinction to elu-
cidate the functioning of churchly sacrament and divine
grace in the process of salvation. That Aquinas had not
chosen to distinguish the two powers in this connection is
surely no accident. For him, the sacraments possessed by
divine endowment an intrinsic, instrumental causality mediating their effects, "a supernatural virtue given to them by
God that enabled them to effect grace in the recipient."[66] For
him, too, the divine grace thus conferred became very much
an integral part of its recipient—in scholastic jargon, an infused habit or accidental form.[67] For so many of the theologians who came after him, however—Scotus, Ockham,
Pierre d'Ailly, and others who trod in Ockham's footsteps—
all of this, while not admittedly making God a debtor to man,
seemed in some way to impugn the divine freedom by making God a debtor to himself, by trapping him within the
salvific arrangements he had himself established, by obliging
him to respond with his saving love to those who, endowed
by the sacraments with the infused habit of grace, themselves strove to love him. To them, in other words, "Thomist
theology seemed to run the danger of entangling the divine
will in the secondary causation of the church, priests, sacraments, and accidental forms of grace."[68] Hence their central
emphasis on the freely willed, chosen, covenantal nature of
the whole machinery of salvation—an approach that had the
advantage of underlining the orderliness of God's workings,
while reinterpreting in a radically antinecessitarian manner
what it means for there to be an order to his actions. Of his
absolute power, he could confer salvation without the presence in the soul of an infused habit of grace or could render
the sacraments incapable of producing such grace. Even *de*

potentia ordinata, moreover, while the sacraments do mediate grace to the soul, they do so not by any intrinsic causal efficacy comparable to natural causality but simply by functioning as conditions *sine qua non,* in a fashion similar (to invoke the analogy the theologians so often use) to the intrinsically worthless leaden coin that the king proclaims himself willing to redeem for a large sum of money.[69] No more than any other of the traditional religious institutions do such arrangements form some "essential link in a great hierarchical chain of being."[70] They are just cogs in the machinery of divine salvation, and if they continue to function as such, that simply reflects the fact that God, who knows no absolute necessity, has freely chosen to bind himself by what Chaucer accurately designates in the *Nun's Priest's Tale* as a "necessitee condicionel"—an "unfailing necessity . . . appropriate to God," as one nominalist theologian put it, "because of his promise, that is, his covenant, or established law [*ex promisso suo et pacto sive lege statuta*]."[71]

Such sentiments are comprehensible enough, of course, in the context of discussions of the economy of salvation, and they are buttressed by biblical references to Yahweh's covenantal relationship with his chosen people. But behind it all looms the theological axiom (so emphasized by Ockham and such sympathizers as d'Ailly) that "whatever God can produce by means of secondary causes he can without them directly produce and conserve,"[72] an axiom with a pertinence extending far beyond the economy of salvation and reaching out to touch the world of natural phenomena and, as a result, the foundations of human knowledge. And given all the affiliated talk about the working of God's absolute power, about miraculous interpositions in the course of nature, most notoriously (and especially so in the case of Ockham) about the possible production in us *de potentia dei absoluta* of intuitions of nonexisting objects,[73] one is prompted to ask whether the late-medieval vogue of the distinction between the absolute and ordained powers may not well have served also to discredit the very possibility of a truly reliable empirical knowledge of the natural world and to impede thereby the development of a viable science of nature.

Chapter 3

NEBUCHADNEZZAR'S FIERY FURNACE

> Our God whom we serve is able to deliver
> us from the burning fiery furnace; and he
> will deliver us out of your hand, O king.
> —Daniel 3:17

I

Science and theology: had it fallen to my lot to address the topic a century ago, the odds are that the smoke of battle would have hung low over my discourse, that my sentences would have clanked with the metaphors of military engagement, that my concern above all would have been to report on the dispositions of the opposing forces locked in combat along a very clearly drawn front. Even today, despite the early-twentieth-century deflation of earlier euphoric and essentially scientistic claims and the concomitant emergence of a much less optimistic estimate of the reach of human reason, despite the subsequent decades of historical revisionism, the growing sophistication in our perceptions of the nature of

67

scientific thinking and of its relation to other modes of intellectual discourse—even today, despite all of these developments and others, too, it remains true of a considerable number of us that the most immediate impression generated by
the juxtaposition of the words "science" and "theology" is
one of tension or conflict. We think, perhaps, of Giordano
Bruno, martyr, it was said, in the cause of an infinite universe. Or of Galileo's "And yet it moves"—his moment of
(apocryphal) defiance before his persecutors. Or of the famous
confrontation on the Darwinian theory which occurred at
Oxford in 1860 between "Darwin's bulldog," Thomas Henry
Huxley, and Samuel Wilberforce, bishop of Oxford, known in
his own day as "Soapy Sam" and described more recently as
"one of those men whose moral and intellectual fibres have
been permanently loosened by the early success and applause
of a distinguished undergraduate career."[1]

All this is true enough. But then we would do well to
remember that the perception of the relationship between
science and theology in the seventeenth century as being
overwhelmingly one of conflict and warfare was very much
of a late-nineteenth-century contribution,[2] popularized in
this country by two widely read American writers. Thus, in
1875, John W. Draper (who in 1860 had delivered a warm-up
speech at the Huxley-Wilberforce encounter) published his
History of the Conflict between Religion and Science—the
title being an accurate indicator of the contents.[3] A year
later, Andrew D. White, president of Cornell University, began the first version of what was to develop into his *History
of the Warfare of Science with Theology* with the following
words:

> I purpose to present an outline of the great sacred struggle for
> the liberty of science—a struggle which has lasted for so many
> centuries, and which yet continues. A hard contest it has
> been; a war waged longer, with battles fiercer, with sieges

more persistent, with strategy more shrewd than in any of the comparatively transient warfare of Caesar or Napoleon or Moltke.

I shall ask you to go with me through some of the most protracted sieges, and over some of the hardest fought battle-fields of this war. We will look well at the combatants; we will listen to the battle-cries; we will note the strategy of leaders, the cut and thrust of champions, the weight of missiles, the temper of weapons.[4]

And so on—and on, eventually, in fact, over two long volumes in which he worked out the military metaphor in almost lugubrious detail, descending from strategy to tactics, from tactics to logistics, from logistics to communications and command infrastructure, right down as it were to battalion, company, and platoon level on the physicotheological front.

These men were among the very first of historians to attempt an assessment of the relationship of science and religion in the seventeenth century. And the picture they painted is, by and large, one of a gloriously emergent natural science triumphing finally over the suffocating superstition and theological obscurantism that was the legacy of the Middle Ages. In this endeavor they betrayed very clearly the impact on their historical thinking of their own involvement in the struggle between the advocates of the Darwinian theory and the defenders of biblical fundamentalism, and they have since been accused, understandably enough, of having projected upon the recalcitrant contours of the seventeenth-century scene the outlines of a problem that was essentially of late-nineteenth-century vintage.

Of course, some of their twentieth-century successors have left themselves open to similar charges.[5] But most have striven to adopt a more purely and self-consciously historical stance than their nineteenth-century predecessors and have admittedly gone a long way toward achieving a balanced,

mediating position that gives adequate recognition to the
degree of religious reinforcement that so many of the early-
modern scientists, from Galileo to Newton, found in their
work, without ignoring or downplaying the fear and tension
that emerged when Christian traditionalists of one sort or
another first felt "the touch of the cold philosophy."[6] A remarkable number of the practitioners of the new science,
after all, were deeply religious men. Focusing on the culmi-
nating phase of the seventeenth-century scientific revolution
when England was at center stage, one thinks immediately of
Robert Boyle or the great Newton himself. Nearly all of these
scientific *virtuosi* (as they were often called),[7] along with
such ideological fellow travelers as Joseph Glanvill and Sir
Thomas Browne, were prone to insist, often at tedious
length, that the created world was a natural revelation of God
and that scientists uncovering the secrets of the natural
world were in a real sense evangelists proclaiming to mankind the glory and might of the Creator.

At the same time, and even as late as 1670, Henry Stubbe
could launch a truly vitriolic attack upon the scientists. In a
group of pamphlets published in that year he attacked the
efforts of the Royal Society in London as "detrimental to
religion" and charged that it was "destroying the weapons
with which Christianity had been defended. . . . The concept
of a mechanical, geometric universe threatened the primacy
of God in the creation. If the Lord be regulated by the rules of
geometry and mechanical motion in the government of the
world, he declared, 'I cannot any way comprehend how God
can do any miracles.'"[8] It has since been established that
Stubbe was a bit of a fraud, a hired hand paid by the Royal
College of Physicians (fearful of the growing prestige of the
Royal Society) to play unscrupulously upon popular fears.[9]
But that fact itself attests to the continued existence of such
fears—as also does the decision of Robert Boyle to provide in

his will for the endowment of a lecture series to be devoted to
the defense of religion.

In the light of these circumstances, it is understandable
that some even of the more recent commentators have been
disposed to question the wisdom of the sentiments expressed
by the *virtuosi* and the accuracy of their judgment when they
spoke so glowingly of the harmony between theology and
science.[10] The *virtuosi* were profoundly mistaken in their
physicotheological rhapsodizings. In pursuing their scientific
investigations they wrought better or worse (depending on
one's point of view)—certainly other than they knew. As
intellectual developments in the eighteenth century were to
show, it was only a matter of time before the incompatibility
of their scientific philosophizing with the traditional structures of Christian belief would become only too lamentably
apparent.

Of course to argue in this fashion, however persuasively,
is once again to leave oneself open to the charge of subor-
dinating the complexities of seventeenth-century intellectual life to the problematic of another era—though this time
not so much of the nineteenth or twentieth century as of the
eighteenth. Throughout the seventeenth century, after all,
the factors promoting the sort of religious skepticism and
secularization of knowledge that were to be such prominent
features of eighteenth-century intellectual life were both multiple and various. It would be easy enough to mount a reason-
ably cogent argument to the effect that the new scientific
philosophy did not bulk all that large among those factors—
even though religious skeptics could claim to find support in
it for their own positions. I do not intend, however, to mount
such an argument. My concern lies elsewhere and at one
remove. It is grounded in the strong sense that the reading of
these seventeenth-century intellectual phenomena in terms
of eighteenth-century culminations persistently disposes one

to view the theological moments of such men as Boyle and
Newton as residual bric-a-brac carried over from an age of
more secure belief, or, at best, as witnessing to their piety as
believers rather than expressing their convictions as scientists.[11]

II

We begin, then, with the views of these more recent
commentators and with Robert Boyle himself—the Boyle of
Boyle's law, the scientist who did so much "to incorporate
chemistry into natural philosophy" and to win for it from the
physicists the recognition that it was "a real and important
science" working in much the same way as their own;[12] the
Boyle whom it is possible without exaggeration to describe as
"the great father figure of British natural philosophy in his
time," and whose foundation "of lectures in 1691 for the
defense of religion . . . began the process of establishing
Newtonianism in Europe;"[13] the Boyle, again, or so his biog-
rapher tells us, who "had so profound a veneration for the
Deity that the very name of God was never mentioned by
him without a pause and a visible stop in his discourse."[14]
The choice of Boyle, then, is a justifiable one, and, given
the amount of time and effort he devoted in his writings to
exploring matters "physico-theological" and to illustrating
what he called the "Reconcileableness of Reason and Religion,"[15] it is understandable that historians have been very
interested in what he made of the relationship between the
new science and the traditional religion. He titled one of his
books *The Christian Virtuoso: Showing that, by being ad-
dicted to Experimental Philosophy, a man is rather assisted
than indisposed to be a good Christian*,[16] and, as that title
indicates, he himself did not appear to believe that there was
anything problematic in the relationship. While some of his

more recent commentators have been willing to take such
assurances at face value,[17] others have not.[18] Seeing the central bone of contention between the natural philosophers and
the Christian traditionalists to be the question of God's relationship to the universe and the nature of his activity within
it, they find his extensive analyses of that topic, of the operation of divine providence and the status of miracles, to be
neither persuasive nor fully coherent. Failing to perceive
"the sceptical implications of the new [idea of] nature," they
argue, Boyle, in company with many another virtuoso, was
swept remorselessly into "a reinterpretation of theism."[19]
The meteorological conditions might seem tranquil enough,
but Boyle's intellectual voyage was in fact an unhappy and
turbulent one, distinguished by somewhat desperate dialectical improvisations and headed ultimately for logical ship-
wreck. "Boyle's opinion about miracles," we are told, "stood
in absolute contradiction to the rest of his thought. It was an
arbitrary and artificial reconciliation of two positions that
could not be reconciled satisfactorily"[20]—namely, his scientific view of the world as a great machine possessed of an
unchanging order and his Christian commitment to belief in
the providential activity of a personal God. For that commitment involved belief not merely in the general divine concourse whereby God sustains in being the whole order of the
universe, but also in those particular providences whereby
God interferes with that order and touches the lives of
individuals.

Other points of tension there doubtless were. But this, we
are told, was the truly central issue, and Boyle's failure was
symptomatic. Throughout the seventeenth century, the *virtuosi* were condemned to fight an increasingly desperate and
ultimately doomed rear-guard action. Maneuver frantically
though they might, they proved unable finally to reconcile
their biblical notion of an all-powerful, loving, and personal
God, from whose providential purview not even the fall of a

sparrow escapes and against whose miraculous intervention not even the might of a Nebuchadnezzar was proof, with their own scientific understanding of the universe as a great and wondrous machine, grinding on its inexorable course in accordance with those immutable and necessary uniformities to which they gave the name of laws of nature and which they took it to be their task as scientists to identify. In the celebrated Clarke-Leibniz correspondence of the years 1715 and 1716, Dr. Samuel Clarke, Newton's apologist, might splutter angrily at Leibniz' sneering intimations that the Newtonians were being inconsistent with their own mechanistic principles in teaching the possibility, indeed the necessity, of God's intervention in the world of nature after creation in order to reform the motions of the planets, perhaps also to conserve the total amount of motion in the world.[21] But Leibniz was correct; he had identified the central dilemma. The story of the relationship between science and religion in the seventeenth century was, in its most fundamental aspect, the story of the progressive exile of the sovereign God of Abraham, Isaac, and Jacob to the remote and inaccessible post of First Cause—the First Cause to which eighteenth-century deists were to accord a thin and sanitized respect and their atheistic colleagues to dismiss as an embarrassing redundancy or a comic obsolescence.

Told in this way, as a story of progressive secularization and with its eighteenth-century culmination and Leibniz' viewpoint positioned well to the foreground, this stretch of history takes on an impressive coherence. As Franklin Baumer has said, "it is a fascinating thing to watch this *reductio* [whereby "divine activity in nature was significantly reduced if not eliminated"] proceed, almost ineluctably it would seem, from Galileo to Newton and Leibnitz."[22] The question remains, however, if that story would look at all the same were one to set it in the context not of what came after but of what went before, of the struggle of the medieval theologians, not, indeed, with any mechanistic philosophy of the seventeenth-century type, but with deterministic or quasi-deterministic notions of neoplatonic and Aristotelian provenance. And the urgency of switching precisely to that tack becomes very evident if one glances at the sort of arguments Boyle typically makes in fighting his alleged rear-guard action, in attempting his "arbitrary and artificial reconciliation" of irreconcilable religious and scientific positions. For what, after all, does he say? He tells us, among other things, that God is "the supreme and absolute lord" of creation, who "established those rules of motion, and that order among things corporeal which we are wont to call the laws of nature."[23] He points out that "the laws of motion, without which the present state and course of things could not be maintained, did not necessarily spring from the nature of matter, but depended upon the will of the divine author of things."[24] He insists that this "present state and course of things"—which he refers to also as "the ordinary or usual course of things" and as "the instituted order"[25]—can be invalidated by God, who, being omnipotent, can "do whatever involves no contradiction."[26] He concludes that "though some modern philosophers have made ingenious attempts to explain the nature of things corporeal, yet their explications generally suppose the present fabric of the world, and the laws of motion that are settled in it."[27]

Hence, when he turns to the question of God's continuing activity in the world, it is hardly surprising that Boyle should insist that ever since "the primordial constitution of things," God, "by his ordinary and general concourse," sustains "those powers, which he gave the parts of matter, to transmit their motion thus and thus to one another."[28] Nor that he should note that miracles involve departures from that "ordinary and general concourse," being "extraordinary and supernatural interpositions of divine providence" by which God may be seen to "over-rule, or controul, the established course of things in the world, by his own omnipotent hand."[29] Nor, more particularly now, that he should argue that

> if we consider God as the author of the universe, and the free establisher of the laws of motion, whose general concourse is necessary to the conservation and efficacy of every particular physical agent, we cannot but acknowledge, that, by withholding his concourse, or changing these laws of motion, which depend perfectly upon his will, he may invalidate most, if not all the axioms and theorems of natural philosophy: these supposing the course of nature. . . . It is a rule in natural philosophy, that *causae necessariae semper agunt quantum possunt;* but it will not necessarily follow from thence, that the fire must necessarily burn Daniel's three companions, or their clothes, that were cast by the Babylonian king's command into the midst of a burning fiery furnace, when the author of nature was pleased to withdraw his concourse to the operation of the flames, or supernaturally to defend against them the bodies, that were exposed to them. . . . Agreeably to this, let me observe to you, that, though it be unreasonable to believe a miraculous effect when attributed only to a mere physical agent, yet the same thing may reasonably be believed, when ascribed to God, or to agents assisted with his absolute or supernatural power.[30]

By now, I trust, all of this is familiar enough—the general line of argument about God's activity *ad extra,* the crucial distinction between his absolute and ordinary powers evoked in order to clarify that line of argument, even the particular biblical incident employed to illustrate it (and Boyle recurs to that incident on two other occasions). If the dialectical weaponry Boyle deploys here is to be labeled as "arbitrary and artificial," it can scarcely be described as original. If he is fighting a rear-guard action, he appears to be doing so within the terms of a tradition of philosophical and theological discourse dating back already in his own day for three centuries and more. If, of course, he is to be understood as fighting a rear-guard action at all. But then, the degree to which his publicistic endeavor can helpfully be pictured in that fashion can best be determined, I believe, by viewing that endeavor from the perspective of the tradition of discourse on which he is drawing.

III

It will be recalled that the distinction that Boyle employs in its updated form had had its origin in the attempts of the early scholastic theologians fully to honor the goodness and wisdom of God without being led thereby, in the unhappy footsteps of Abelard, to impose limits on his freedom and omnipotence. It will be recalled, too, that the arena of debate (and the arena, therefore, within which the distinction between the absolute or ordained powers of God came into play) was that of the order of creation. That is to say, the questions that were generating the difficulty probed the matter of the divine omnipotence by raising such issues as God's capacity to create a different or better world than he had actually created. And Albertus Magnus and Aquinas sought to vindicate the divine omnipotence by arguing that of his freedom and from an infinity of possibilities God had chosen to create a world that is in accord with his goodness and wisdom. But perhaps it will be recalled also that, in the wake of the thirteenth-century reception of Aristotle and of the theological reaction of which the condemnations of 1277 were as much symptom as cause, the arena of debate came to be widened and the reach of the distinction between the divine powers lengthened.

Thus, in an attempt to protect the biblical doctrine of God against the philosophical necessitarianism or determinism that appeared at least to many to be part and parcel of Aristotle's thought, philosophers and theologians in the fourteenth

and fifteenth centuries were led to place a heightened emphasis on God's freedom and omnipotence, in relation not only
to his creation of the world but also to his governance of
created things. Hence, when the distinction between the absolute and ordained powers was invoked (as it was with in-
creasing frequency), the line tended to be drawn between the
ordained, ordinary, or common law in accord with which
God condescends to work within the framework he has established and the absolute power whereby he can do anything that does not involve a contradiction—whereby, therefore, he can transcend (and on occasion has transcended) that
established order.

Pressed too hard, of course, this emphasis carries with it
the danger of evoking the vision of a world so thoroughly
impregnated by the divine will that the very idea of a natural
order becomes a quasi-blasphemous intrusion. Already in the
tenth century, moved by similar religious worries in the Islamic world, Al Ash'arī and his followers appear to have
arrived at a position close to that. In their attempts to protect
the freedom and omnipotence of God, the Asharites had
adopted an atomistic view of things, denied the necessity of
cause and effect, ignored the idea of natural law, and made
God directly responsible for everything that happens at every
moment of time. In a world thus conceived, in which all
"natural" processes were at best sacramental rather than natural,[31] there could be no threat to the freedom and omnipotence of God, but little room also for that instinctive confidence in the existence of a stable and rational natural order
without which the natural sciences, as A. N. Whitehead once
argued, could scarcely have developed.[32] Of the early-medi-
eval theologians of Latin Christendom, St. Peter Damiani, as
we have seen, showed some sympathy with such a position.
Of the late-medieval nominalists, one at least, Nicholas of
Autrecourt in the fourteenth century, appears, though by a
different route, to have come even closer, denying natural

causality and embracing, as did the Asharites, a form of atomism.[33]

It was once common to assume that Nicholas was a faithful follower of William of Ockham, but we now know this not to have been the case. Nicholas, in this respect at least, was a much more radical thinker.[34] He appears to have admitted no distinction between the absolute and ordained powers of God, and it was for his refusal to concede in natural philosophy the adequacy or validity of empirical arguments *ex suppositione*—that is, arguments based on the assumption of a natural order established by God's ordained power, or, if I may be permitted anachronistically to use Boyle's words, arguments based on the assumption of "the present fabric of the world and the laws of motion that are settled in it"—it was for his refusal to admit the validity of such arguments that he was criticized by John Buridan, the nominalist philosopher-scientist. Buridan regarded Nicholas, he said, as wishing "to destroy the natural and moral sciences,"[35] and as a result, in his capacity as rector of the University of Paris, authorized in 1340 the condemnation of some of his views.[36] Their discrimination of an ordained power whereby God acts in accordance with the laws he himself has established in his creation enabled such nominalist philosophers and theologians as Buridan and Ockham to preserve the conviction of a stable and knowable natural order (and of a causality operating *ex natura rei*). But it is now time to note that the degree to which they emphasized the absolute power, while it did not lead them to the radical extremes of the Asharites or of a Nicholas of Autrecourt, did involve a very significant shift in their understanding of the *nature* of that natural order,[37] and one that took them away from that harmonious vision of an immanent and hierarchical order associated with the great chain of being.

In discussing the creation of the universe, Aquinas had followed the trail blazed before him by Augustine and had

retained the Platonic Ideas in their neoplatonic guise as creative archetypes in the mind of God. By so doing he was able
to assert that the creative act was not only a free but also a
rational one, thus vindicating the rationality and intelligibility of the universe. By so doing, however, he was also
led to think of the world of nature in a manner at least cognate to what Collingwood once called "the Greek idea of
nature"—that is, nature viewed as an intelligent organism on
the analogy of the individual human being.[38] As a result,
when he thought of those observable uniformities in natural
occurrences that the early-modern scientists called "laws of
nature," Aquinas conceived of them in Greek fashion as the
external manifestations of an indwelling and immanent
reason.

Aquinas spoke, therefore, of an "eternal law" that orders
to their appropriate end all created things, irrational as well
as rational. Insofar as all things participate in that law, he
understood it to be built, as it were, into their very nature.
Insofar as it was a manifestation of the divine reason, he
understood it also to be grounded in the very Being of God,
and he defined it, therefore, as "nothing other than the idea
of the divine wisdom insofar as it directs all acts and move-
ments" and governs "the whole community of the universe."[39] It is the advantage of this way of looking at things
that it enabled Aquinas to regard the whole of being—including the realm of natural causation as well as that of man's
moral endeavors—as in its own fashion subject to the dictates of the same law. The disadvantage, however, is that
that subjection to law could well be seen to extend to God
himself, thus threatening his freedom and omnipotence,
since the eternal law is nothing other than one aspect of the
divine reason, and in God reason is prior to will.

In the wake of the theological reaction of the late thirteenth century, however, that priority came to be reversed.
However insistent the stress on the fact that in God to will

and to understand are the same, the primacy in God's working *ad extra* was now accorded to the divine will,[40] and the order of the created world (both the moral order governing human behavior and the natural order governing the behavior of irrational beings) came with the nominalists to be understood no longer as a participation in a divine reason that is in some measure transparent to human reason, but as the deliverance of an inscrutable divine will. The doctrine of the divine ideas came under challenge, and with it the whole metaphysic of essences on which it had depended, as well as the affiliated understanding of the universe as an intelligible organism penetrable by *a priori* reasoning precisely because it was moved by an indwelling and immanent reason. The tendency, therefore, was to set God over against the world he had created and which was constantly dependent upon him, to view that world as an aggregate of particular entities linked solely by external relations, each comprehensible in isolation from the others and open to investigation only by empirical endeavor.

The impact of this shift is dramatically evident in the way in which the nominalist thinkers of the fourteenth and fifteenth centuries discussed the ultimate grounding of the moral law. Ockham and d'Ailly are notably explicit on this point, skillfully deploying the distinction between the absolute and ordained powers in such a way as to enable them to ground the content of ethical norms in the divine will while at the same time maintaining the stability and reliability of the moral order and insisting in traditional fashion that there is such a thing as a natural morality made known to all men through that natural law to which right reason is a reliable guide.[41] Thus "evil is nothing other than the doing of something opposite to that which one is obliged to do." Adultery, robbery, hate of God even—all of them in accord with the ordained law (*de communi lege*) vices—could be stripped of their evil and rendered meritorious "if they were to agree

with the divine precept just as now, *de facto,* their opposites
agree with the divine precept.[42] For "God is obliged to the
causing of no act."[43] It is true that, of his ordained power,
God condescends to work within the framework of the moral
law that he has already established, and to which right reason
is our guide, but of his absolute power he is not bound by that
order.[44] The dictates of natural law, the rectitude of right
reason, the very fact that it is virtuous to act in accord with
right reason—all of these amount from the human point of
view to nothing more than inscrutable manifestations of the
divine omnipotence.[45]

More often than not, historians have failed to discriminate this more voluntarist understanding of natural law from
the rationalist version expounded by Aquinas. But it had in
fact a distinct and continuous history stretching right down
to the end of the seventeenth century and beyond. Among its
adherents were numbered not only such scholastics as Jean
Gerson, John Major, and Francisco Suárez (this last in modi-
fied form), or such Protestant theologians as Luther, Zwingli,
Calvin, Ames, and Willard, but such other early-modern lu-
minaries as the early Hugo Grotius (he later changed his
mind), Thomas Hobbes (if he really meant it), the botanist
Nehemiah Grew, and (or so I have argued) that other Fellow
of the Royal Society, John Locke.[46] And mention of the Royal
Society prompts me to note that hand in hand with this
understanding of the moral or juridical natural law as
grounded in the will rather than the reason of God went a
parallel understanding of the order of the physical world, not
as some sort of participation in the divine reason or as immanent in the very natures of things, but as imposed on the
universe, as it were from the outside, by God's sovereign fiat.

While during the later Middle Ages the legal metaphor
was not applied to the world of nature with the clarity and
frequency that by the end of the seventeenth century had
become a commonplace in scientific writings, it was not en-

tirely lacking. Even Ockham, who to my knowledge does not use with a clearly scientific connotation the precise term "laws of nature" or "natural law," does make use of the legal metaphor to indicate the fixed order according to which God of his ordained power acts.[47] And Pierre d'Ailly, who constantly draws comparisons between God's will as "the first obligatory rule or law in the genus of obligating law" and "the first efficient cause in the genus of efficient causality,"[48] employs among others such revealing phrases as "by the common course of nature," "by the common laws and naturally," and "naturally, or by the ordained law."[49] Indeed, he goes further than that and not only speaks of God as having ordained "a natural law" in the things of this world but even, as if to underline the externally imposed nature of that law, admits the relevance to the universe of that clock analogy which was to be popularized in the seventeenth century by Robert Boyle and to become a cliché of eighteenth-century deist theology.[50]

Even when the expression "natural law" or "law of nature" was not used, the idea that it eventually came to denote might well be present.[51] The very distinction between the absolute and ordained powers of God, so closely affiliated with the notion of divinely imposed law, was, as we have seen, applied to the realm of physical occurrence no less than to the ethical sphere or the economy of salvation. And it was so applied not only by theologians concerned to explain how God, by the supernatural interposition of his absolute power, could make miracles (what one might call the Nebuchadnezzar syndrome), but also, so the historians of science tell us, by such fourteenth-century scientists as John Buridan and Marsilius of Inghen as a dialectical tool enabling them to pursue speculative possibilities pertaining to notions of the void, infinity, and the plurality of worlds.[52] And if the natural world that such men studied was no longer conceived as a luminous world fraught with purpose by virtue of its own

indwelling rationality, they did see it, nonetheless, as possessing an order that God by virtue of his ordained power had
freely imposed upon it. And to *that* contingent order, as Buridan insisted against Autrecourt, the empirical investigations
of the scientists, though certainly not proof against the incur-
sions of omnipotence, could be taken to be a safe guide.[53]
God does not play games. Just as in the order of redemption,
the realm of theological causality, God has bound himself by
his covenant with his church to a salvific process that,
though utterly dependent on his will, he will not choose to
change, so, too, by analogy and in the realm of natural
causality, he has bound himself by covenant with the whole
of mankind to sustain the particular order that out of the
unfathomable freedom of his will he has chosen to impose
upon the natural world. The biblical God is not only a God of
power and might; he is also a God who, of his incomprehensible mercy, has condescended to bind himself with prom-
ises.[54]

IV

Evidence abounds to suggest that this covenantal tradition is the appropriate context in which to attempt to understand Robert Boyle's own physicotheological views—certainly more appropriate than a perspective conditioned by
the views of Leibniz or by those of the eighteenth-century
deists. By the seventeenth century "the idea of a pact or
covenant" had for much of the thought of the day, "become a
formative presupposition."[55] When King James I of England
wanted to argue for the notion that a king must frame his
government in accord with what he called the "paction made
to his people by his lawes," he instinctively adduced by way
of analogy "that paction which God made with *Noe* after the
deluge, *Here after Seed-time, and Harvest, Cold and Heate,*

Summer and Winter, and Day and Night shall not cease, so long as the earth remaines."[56] Similarly William Ames evoked the covenantal theme with explicit reference to the physical world when he spoke of "that order in natural things [which] is the law of nature common to all things" and "arises from the force and efficacy of the never revoked word of God given at the beginning. *Let it be made, Let it be, Be it so."*[57] And the distinction between the absolute and ordained powers or extraordinary and ordinary providence of God, itself reflective of the covenantal vision, not only reverberated through the writings of seventeenth-century theologians but generated echoes and harmonics in the thinking of Francis Bacon, Descartes, and Newton.[58]

Even among the scientists, then, whether one has in mind his late-medieval and early-modern predecessors or his contemporaries, there was nothing novel or singular about Boyle's preoccupation with the divine omnipotence. It was part not simply of the religious but also of the philosophical and scientific tradition in which he stood. Twenty and more years ago, in addressing the question of why it was that during the seventeenth century, and after centuries of theological currency, the idea of laws of nature attained a position of such crucial importance in the physical sciences, I suggested that if one focuses on the central thread of scientific development from Galileo and Bacon to Descartes, Boyle, and Newton, the *real* problem, rather, was why, after so many centuries of almost total immersion in Greek ideas of immanent law, the biblical notion of imposed laws of nature burst into such prominence in scientific thinking. I answered that question by pointing out how misleading it was to speak of "*the* medieval view of the world" or "*the* medieval view of natural law," by distinguishing from the general body of natural-law thinking what I have called the *voluntarist* tradition, by describing its emergence in the fourteenth and fifteenth centuries, and by charting its transmission across the ideological

turbulence of the age of Reformation into the crowded arena
of seventeenth-century intellectual life. There it became
something of a cliché, especially among the Protestant theologians, and, among the scientists, powerfully shaped the
thinking of Protestant and Catholic alike.[59]

That solution I find no less compelling today than I did
twenty years ago.[60] In his *Treatise Concerning Immutable
Morality*, to cite a contemporary witness, Ralph Cudworth,
the Cambridge Platonist, signaled his alarm about the re-
emergence in his day of the voluntarist ethic, which he
linked, interestingly enough, with the revival of "the phys-
iological hypotheses of Democritus and Epicurus" (i.e., atomism), and with their successful application "to the solving of
some of the phenomena of the visible world" (i.e., contemporary scientific endeavor). "Though the ancient fathers of the
Christian church were very abhorrent from this doctrine," he
asserted, "yet it crept up afterward in the scholastic age,
Ockham being among the first that maintained . . . that
there is no act evil but as it is prohibited by God, and which
cannot be made good if it be commanded by God." Adding
that "this doctrine hath been since chiefly promoted and
advanced by such as think nothing so essential to the Deity,
as uncontrollable power and arbitrary will," he went on to
single out for special emphasis "that ingenious philosopher
Renatus Descartes."[61]

Cudworth's specific concern, of course, was with the
grounding of ethical norms, but Descartes's marked emphasis on the divine freedom and omnipotence had a wider import. In company with so many of the scientists of his day,
Descartes certainly viewed the laws of nature as imposed on
the world by God just as, he says, "a king establishes laws in
his kingdom," and he goes so far as to make even the truths
of mathematics contingent on the divine will, for such truths
are not to be conceived "to emanate from God like the rays of
the sun." It was, rather, "as the supreme legislator" that God

"ordained them from all eternity." Accordingly, though the very idea defies any merely human comprehension, if he so willed he could change those laws and render it untrue, for example, that twice four should make eight.[62]

In this, of course, Descartes represents something of an extreme. His stress on the divine omnipotence, indeed, has not always been taken at face value, and some of his contemporaries appear to have regarded him as an atheist. But atheism, said Boyle, who was one of his great (if qualified) admirers, "would subvert the very foundation of those tenets of mechanical philosophy that are particularly his."[63] Other *virtuosi* would clearly have concurred in that judgment. For Walter Charleton, probably one of the "proximate sources" of Boyle's own "corpuscular" (or atomistic) ideas,[64] the "Light of Nature" dispelled "the Darkness of Atheism" and omnipotence was "the Cardinal Prerogative of Divinity." "The ordinary and established laws of nature" were nothing other than God's "ordinary instrument," "rules prescribed by his will," and it would be nothing other than a blasphemous attempt to chain up "his armes in the adamantine fetters of Destiny" if we were to deny him "a *reserved power* of infringing, or altering any one of those laws, which [He] Himself ordained and enacted."[65] Similarly John Locke, who (in his early *Essays on the Law of Nature*) took the notion of God's having imposed his will upon nature in the form of constant laws to be an idea so widely accepted that he used it as a justification for suggesting that man, in his moral life, too, is subject to a natural law.[66] Similarly Sir Isaac Newton, who described God as the Being who "governs all things, not as the soul of the world, but as Lord over all," by his own will imposing laws of nature upon the celestial bodies, "cooperating with all things according to accurate laws . . . except where it is good to act otherwise," and capable of varying "the laws of nature" and of making "worlds of several sorts in several parts of the universe."[67]

In the context of such commitments, the suggestion that
these men in general or Boyle in particular had to wrestle
with some unbearable tension between their commitment to
the traditional Christian teaching on the divine providence
and their scientific vision of the world as a great machine
operating in accord with mechanical laws—that suggestion
takes on a very anachronistic coloration.[68] For it simply ig-
nores the covenantal tradition that sustained their thinking.
In arguing against those whom he called "deists"—that is,
those who claimed that "after the first formation of the universe, all things are brought to pass by the settled laws of
nature"—Boyle not only insisted on the dependency of those
laws "upon the will of the divine author of things," but also
in two fascinating passages conceded that the word "law"
can be applied only in a figurative sense to the behavior of
irrational entities, so that "the actions of inanimate bodies,
which cannot incite or moderate their own actions, are produced by real power, not by laws." For law, he says, is "a
moral, not a physical cause." Though "for brevity's sake" he,
like others, did not scruple to speak of "the laws of nature,"
he noted that strictly speaking law is "but a notional thing,
according to which, an intelligent and free agent is bound to
regulate its actions," such agents alone being able to "regulate the exertions of their power by settled rules."[69] And I
believe that these texts can fittingly be complemented by
placing side by side with them a parallel text in Suárez
where, discussing the distinction between the two powers of
God and defining the ordinary power as that by which God
"operates in accordance with the common laws which he has
established in the universe," he, too, concedes that "things
lacking reason are, properly speaking, capable neither of law
nor of obedience." Accordingly, he goes on to rephrase his
definition of God's ordinary power and describes it now as
that by which he acts "according to the ordinary law which
he has imposed *upon himself*."[70] If Boyle did not explicitly

make this specific dialectical move, the whole tenor of his thought suggests that he would have approved of it entirely.

This being so, then, there was surely no further dialectical strain involved in making room for those exercises of God's particular providence called "miracles" by regarding them as his suspension of his general concourse, that is, his momentary suspension of the "settled rules" for dealing with created things that he had freely chosen to impose on himself. The less so, indeed, if, with Descartes, one is tempted (Damiani fashion) to collapse what he called "God's extraordinary power" into his "ordinary"[71] and to think in terms of the constant recreation of nature "from moment to moment by God's arbitrary will."[72] And no more so if, with Newton, and to allude to the claim that Leibniz ridiculed, "God's *potentia absoluta* was given a new meaning since motion 'is always upon the decay' and planetary irregularities will increase 'till the system wants a reformation.' . . .Just as God preordained that nature could be partly explained by second causes, so he preordained that he would [from time to time] intervene in creation to manifest his power."[73]

With the mention of Leibniz, however, I feel a sharp tug at the tether that binds me to the subject at hand, and I am brought back to the topic of the great chain of being and to Lovejoy, who, it will be recalled, claimed that of all "the great philosophical systems of the seventeenth century," it was in that of Leibniz "that the conception of the Chain of Being is most conspicuous, most determinative, and most pervasive." And who also argued that Leibniz was led thereby so to ground the being of all existents in the necessary order of the divine ideas that, struggle though he might to avoid the conclusion, he proved unable in the end to avoid the sort of determinism characteristic of the system of Spinoza.[74]

Now it is one of the interesting facets of all the talk about omnipotence in the scientists I have been discussing that it is

rather self-consciously linked with the need to reject any
trace of necessity either in God or in the world he has created. Thus Charleton contrasts God's "arbitrary activity" in
the world with "Fate in the notion of the Stoicks,"[75] and
Descartes assures us that to say that mathematical truths
were independent of God's will would be to speak of him as a
Jupiter or a Saturn and to subject him to the Fates.[76] Thus
Roger Cotes, in the preface to the second edition of Newton's
Principia, tells us that in the laws of nature that flow from
"the perfectly free Will of God . . . appear many traces indeed of the most wise contrivance but not the least shadow
of necessity."[77] Thus Boyle, pondering the old scholastic
question concerning God's ability to make a better world
than he in fact had created, and evoking God's "immense
power and unexhausted wisdom," answered in contrast both
to Abelard and to Leibniz that "the divine architect" could
indeed "make [such] a greater master-piece." Or again, citing
the Aristotelian denial to God of either the creation or the
providential government of the world, confessed that he took
"divers of *Aristotle's* opinions relating to religion to be more
unfriendly, not to say pernicious, to it, than those of several
other heathen philosophers"—and it is clear that what he had
in mind were the atomist views of those he called the "Epicurean and other corpuscularian infidels."[78]

That is a claim, had they known about it, that Al-Asharī
or Al-Ghazālī, centuries earlier, could happily have endorsed.
It is a claim, too, or so I like to believe, in which Lovejoy, too,
would have concurred. But when it came to the early-modern
scientists, Lovejoy's interests lay elsewhere—with Bruno, or
Leibniz, or William Derham, or the great naturalist John Ray,
men who sympathized with the notion of the great chain of
being or with one or other of its component ideas. And it was
in effect against sympathizers with such notions that Boyle
was also writing when he raised his criticism of Aristotle.
His worries about the imposition of limits and restrictions
on God's activity in the world were certainly faithful echoes

of a centuries-old tradition of worry about the threat that some of Aristotle's ideas posed to religious orthodoxy, Muslim no less than Christian.[79] But central though Aristotle was to those worries they did not alone concern him or his medieval followers. They responded also to the concept of plastic nature defended by such Cambridge Platonists as Henry More, to the notion that in creating the material substratum of the world God did not leave it totally passive and inert but infused it instead with a vital spiritual power, at once both formative and directive and immediately responsible across time for the multiple configurations of natural entities.[80] More broadly, they responded to the popularity even within the scientific community of that complex of views which Boyle labeled as "the vulgarly received notion of nature," with its immanentism, its hierarchical vision, its assertion of the indwelling of reason or spirit in nature, and its concomitant ascription to nature of some sort of independence of God as his "intelligent and powerful" (if subordinate) "viceregent."[81] Or again, its postulation of "plastic principles," world souls, "substantial forms," "separate agents," "spiritual intelligences," active intermediaries between God and the Universe that detract from the nobility of his stature as "the sovereign Lord and Governor of the world."[82]

It was in response to Johann Christoph Sturm's defense of the mechanical view of nature for which Boyle had argued in his "Free Inquiry" that Leibniz in 1698 wrote his own *De ipsa natura, sive de vi insita, actionibusque creaturarum.* But while in that work he rejects as "partly impossible, partly superfluous" Henry More's "hylarchic principle" (in effect, the "vulgarly received notion of nature" that Boyle also rejects),[83] at the same time he is quite explicit in finding Boyle's apparatus of mechanical forces and imposed laws inadequate to explain the nature and behavior of things. That approach, with its externalism, its fixation on "the divine volition and command," smacks for him of Malebranchian occasionalism.[84] It simply does not suffice. What is needed, and *pace* both Boyle and Sturm, is the recognition of the presence within the world of natural things of a created but "indwelling active force," and "indwelling law" (*lex insita*) "from which actions and passions proceed."[85] And via that route Leibniz is led to refurbish the notion of substantial form, to signal that he thinks Aristotle's profundity to have been underestimated,[86] to ascribe to natural phenomena a certain independence of God and to things once created a certain "self-sustaining efficacy."[87]

I am led, then, to advance a suggestion and to propose a question. The suggestion looks back to the portrayal of a Leibniz who, in his opening confrontation with Samuel Clarke and his criticism of Newton for arguing that God would have to intervene in the universe from time to time, was in effect doing nothing other than urging upon the Newtonians the logical conclusion of their own mechanical principles. Such a portrayal is, I believe, anachronistic and mistaken. I suggest, instead, that we would do better to think of the Clarke-Leibniz confrontation as an encounter between two men each possessed of one of the radically different understandings of the nature of things that are to be found jostling side by side in early-modern scientific thinking.[88] The one, that of Leibniz, redolent of the view encapsulated in Lovejoy's great chain of being. The other, Clarke's, responding, rather, to what I have called the covenantal vision. As for the question, which looks forward to the next chapter, it is stimulated by the fact that in responding to Leibniz, who had ridiculed Newton's God as an incompetent watchmaker, Clarke portrayed Leibniz' God as a do-nothing king.[89] Such God-king parallelisms, it turns out, are very common in the theological and scientific literature I have been discussing. But what is one to make of them? Are they mere rhetorical flourishes, or should one attach to them some deeper significance?[90]

Chapter 4

DIVINE SOVEREIGNTY, PAPAL MIRACLE, ROYAL GRACE

> The Power of the Supreme Potentate and Monarch of
> England is doble and devided into two braunches,
> the one Absolute and the other Ordinate.
> —Sir John Doddridge

I

At its broadest, the historical context of what follows is that of the rise of constitutional forms of government—that is, those forms of government that, as a matter of course and in accordance with recognized and stable legal norms, limit the use of executive power by measures short of force. More narrowly, the context is that of the constitutional climate of early-modern Europe, where absolute monarchy was coming increasingly to be regarded as the truly *modern* thing, the only *civilized* form of government, where the traditional medieval limitations on monarchical power were coming to be dismissed as "inefficient clogs upon the wheels of government," as "not merely wrong but stupid,"[1] and where, accordingly, the representative institutions that had flourished throughout medieval Europe were lapsing into desuetude.

And the most immediate perspective is framed by the fact that it was in England, and in England alone, that medieval representative institutions survived at the national level to become the direct foundation of a modern constitutionalist and parliamentary regime, serving, moreover, at one or another remove, properly or improperly understood, as the model for so many other representative constitutionalist regimes in the modern world.

In view of this fact, here too, as earlier in the story of the rise of modern science, a considerable importance attaches to the England of the seventeenth century. Though, in this case, that importance attaches to the course of English constitutional history of the first half of the seventeenth century, the period when England slid into constitutional crisis and civil war, and when the very survival of the traditional constitutional limitations on monarchical power appeared to be at stake. And, again, that importance attaches less to the great clash of hostile armies than to the clash of competing political and constitutional theories that both presaged and accompanied it—even to those distressingly foggy discussions of the royal prerogative and the king's emergency powers which so alarmed English parliamentarians of the seventeenth century, which have so exasperated English constitutional historians of the twentieth, but which contrive so to intrigue people who, like myself, are fascinated by ideas and their history.

It is not that historians of political thought have traditionally taken a great deal of interest in the doctrine of the divine right of kings which impinged upon these discussions of the prerogative. Just as the physicotheological claims of a Robert Boyle came to seem strained and untenable when read anachronistically through later Leibnizian or deist lenses, so the divine right of kings when seen in the light of the Glorious Revolution of 1688 and the subsequent triumph of the constitutionalist vision. And historians of political thought have tended persistently (if, again, anachronistically) to see it in that light. Their bone-deep, Whiggish conviction of its essential absurdity was such as to inhibit the development of any such interest—so much so, indeed, that for long, and in the teeth of Locke's explicit statements to the contrary, they were wont to insist that the true target of that thinker's *Two Treatises of Government* was Thomas Hobbes and not the version of the divine right theory expounded by Sir Robert Filmer in his *Patriarcha: A Defence of the Natural Power of Kings against the Unnatural Power of the People*.[2] As John Neville Figgis wrote about ninety years ago in his pioneering book on the subject (and echoing the words of a distinguished contemporary), "never has there been a doctrine better written *against* than the Divine Right of Kings."[3]

If that is true of the doctrine in general, it is even truer of the particular expression given to it in the writings of King James VI of Scotland and James I of England, which fill 345 pages in the 1918 edition by Charles Howard McIlwain.[4] "In his prime," James I "was admired . . . as a man of intelligence, of dignity and of pleasing appearance. He was not the buffoon in purple or the impossible pedant that the scandalmongers of the court would have us believe."[5] But his vanity, bad manners, obsessive fear of assassination, the difficulty he encountered in trying to fit English institutions and practices to his native Scottish preconceptions, his propensity, nonetheless, for lecturing royal advisers and parliaments alike on the mysteries of statecraft, as well as the laziness, slovenliness, physical deterioration, and growing insobriety that characterized his later years—all of these have lent enough color to the caricature as to leave his writings obscured by the shadow of his reputation as "the wisest fool in Christendom."[6] As a result, even his less unsympathetic modern commentators have tended mainly to stress not the broader theoretical framework of those writings but the historical and legal arguments for the indefeasible character of the royal authority to be found in them.[7]

During the past twenty-five years, however, largely because of the work of W. H. Greenleaf, the realization has dawned "that James's political thought was neither so simple nor so foolish" as it has often been made to appear, that "he deserves a higher place in the history of systematic political thought" than he has normally been accorded, and that so, too, "does the set of [divine right] ideas of which he was so able a proponent."[8] And, as Greenleaf also points out, both that set of ideas in general and his own political thinking in particular find succinct and representative expression in the celebrated (or notorious) speech which the king delivered to both houses of Parliament on March 21, 1609, and which, he says, is "central to an understanding of James's political theory."[9]

II

We take our point of departure, then, from that event, which occurred in the context of an unhappy conjunction between a royal request for additional and substantial financial supply and an outburst of parliamentary irritation at the extravagant claims for the royal prerogative which Dr. John Cowell, professor of civil law at Cambridge, had made in a recently published book.[10] Having warmed up his audience with an outline of the topics he intended to address, James launched into his discourse with the following passage:

> The state of MONARCHIE is the supremest thing upon earth: For Kings are not onely GODS Lieutenants upon earth, and sit upon GODS throne, but even by GOD himselfe they are called Gods. There bee three principall similitudes that illustrates

the state of MONARCHIE: One taken out of the word of God; and the other two out of the grounds of Policie and Philosophie. In the Scriptures Kings are called Gods, and so their power after a certaine relation compared to the Divine power. Kings are also compared to Fathers of families: for a King is trewly *Parens patriae,* the politique father of his people. And lastly, Kings are compared to the head of this Microcosme of the body of man.

Having laid that groundwork, James went on to draw from the first of his three correspondences (the God-king parallel), and in the most abrasive terms, some very forthright conclusions concerning the reach of his own royal power. "Kings," he said,

are justly called Gods, for they exercise a manner or resemblance of Divine power upon earth: For if you wil consider the Attributes to God, you shall see how they agree in the person of a King. God hath power to create, or destroy, make, or unmake at his pleasure, to give life, or send death, to judge all, and to be judged nor accomptable to none: To raise low things, and to make high things low at his pleasure, and to God are both soule and body due. And the like power have Kings: they make and unmake their subjects: they have power of raising, and casting downe: of life, and of death: Judges over all their subjects, and in all causes, and yet accomptable to none but God onely. They have power to exalt low things, and abase high things, and make of their subjects like men at the Chesse.[11]

These were not, admittedly, sentiments designed to warm the hearts of the restive parliamentarians, many of them practitioners of the common law, who had little choice but to grind their teeth and listen. But they were sentiments, nonetheless, that aroused in Greenleaf a scholarly excitation akin to that of the hound whose nostrils have suddenly caught the scent of a truly worthwhile quarry. For in those

words he saw expressed, as it were *in nuce,* the very philosophical foundation of James's whole theory of divine right.
That foundation, he argued, was "derived from a range of
metaphysical notions which collectively may be called 'the
idea of order'." That idea he regarded as "best described,"
even classically so, in Lovejoy's *Great Chain of Being,* and its
imprint on the literature (though not, alas, the political
thinking) of the sixteenth and seventeenth centuries as well
delineated in a whole series of distinguished studies, notably
E. M. W. Tillyard's *Elizabethan World Picture.*[12]

Thus God was seen as having created "a great chain of
being," a "single ascending scale of things from the lowest
form of material existence to the highest manifestation of
the purely spiritual." "Man himself was regarded as the piv-
otal link in the chain; with both a soul and body he shared
uniquely in both its spiritual and material aspects thus constituting a microcosm of the whole"; like that whole himself
hierarchically organized, with the faculty of reason at the
summit and controlling all.[13] And the societies that men
formed, if ordered properly in reflection of those macrocosmic and microcosmic patterns, at once both rational
and divine, must likewise be hierarchically organized, with
subjects disposed in their several rankings and degrees, ascending up to the monarch, whose oneness of being and absoluteness of power undergirds the unity and stability of the
whole. In this, of course, his role is directly analogous to that
of God in relation to the universe, and, in terms of "this
framework of ideas" in general, a special urgency and importance attaches to the "'argument by correspondence', the
elaboration of often very complex analogies between different planes of the scale of being so that the understanding of
one part of it could be improved by what was known of
another."[14]

Only with "this background in mind," Greenleaf argued,
could the political writings of James I be "properly under-

stood."[15] Similarly, such other influential formulations of divine right theory as Edward Forset's *Comparative Discourse of the Bodies Natural and Politique,* which was published in 1606, or Filmer's *Patriarcha,* written probably between 1635 and 1642 but published for the first time in 1680.[16] This "political theory of order" being, in effect, a harmonic reflection of the world view associated with the great chain of being, there was clearly nothing particularly novel about it and Greenleaf finds it in the theological and political writings of Thomas Aquinas, among earlier thinkers. But whereas in Aquinas, he notes, it was linked with an insistence on the limited nature of political authority and the concession that "in certain circumstances there was a right of resistance," by the seventeenth century it had come to be placed at the service of very different ends. Such was its conceptual flexibility, indeed, that the seventeenth-century royalists were able to use it to support "the absolute nature" and "untrammelled sovereign power" of kings as well as the belief that "rebellion was never justified even against an evil and tyrannous ruler."[17] Moral limits to the exercise of royal power this philosophy of order continued, of course, to affirm and support, but, in its seventeenth-century royalist version at least, it proscribed any concrete external means of imposing such limits on a ruler. "And, as Hobbes sagely observed, a self-imposed limitation is really no limitation at all."[18]

Thus Greenleaf, and thus the case rested until five years ago. Since then, James Daly, a Canadian scholar, has entered the lists with a trio of richly documented studies—one on Filmer, one on the meaning of "absolutism" or "absolute monarchy" in seventeenth-century England, and one on what he calls "the Elizabethan picture of cosmic harmony" and which he describes as having informed the political thinking of the sixteenth and early seventeenth centuries.[19] It is not his purpose to challenge Greenleaf's basic claim that the world view associated with the notion of the great chain of being forms the essential philosophical foundation for royalist divine-right theories, lending them for contemporaries much of their cogency and persuasive power. Far from it. He wishes instead to endorse that claim, paying tribute the while to Lovejoy's "seminal work" and Greenleaf's happy application of its lessons to the study of political thought. In support of the latter's basic contention, therefore, Daly marshals an impressive body of evidence gleaned by a painstaking canvas of a very broad array of seventeenth-century royalist authors. And he presses the claim for the impregnation of royalist political thinking by the notion of cosmic harmony with a persuasive force and sense of theoretical nuance that succeeds finally in nudging the argument forward beyond the point at which Greenleaf had left it.

Thus a significance attaches even to Daly's adoption of the descriptive term "cosmic harmony." He chose it, he says, instead of "cosmic order," because "*order* may imply commanded or imposed orderliness, whereas *harmony* carries the right note of inherent, natural orderliness, which depends on the nature of things rather than an artificial [that is, imposed] orderliness."[20] At every level in the chain of being, at the divine no less than the human, there was acknowledged the indwelling presence of law. Law conceived, however, not as "arbitrary command representing power, but [as] the expression of an intrinsic necessity, springing from the nature of things, and governing their harmonious operation." Indeed, "one of the keys to the understanding of cosmic harmony [no pun apparently intended] is an apprehension of its relation between reason and will, and its horror of will asserting itself against the order of things which was permeated by a system of degree which reason had discovered."[21] While one of "the deepest consequences" of the Protestant Reformation, Daly concedes, had been at the level of natural theology "a voluntarism which reduced law to the inscrutable will of the divine lawgiver," against such a view the cosmic

harmonists pushed back hard, so that "old and deeply en-
trenched world views remained dominant for much longer."[22] In relation to God's nature, for example, that divine
psychologist Richard Hooker reaffirmed the Thomistic priority of reason to will, and in relation to that analogous and
"corporall god" the king the royalist authors did likewise. As
late as 1679, speaking for "the once universal mentality,"
William Falkner wrote:

> . . . [I]t is neither necessary, nor most suitable to supremacy
> of Government, that the rules by which the Governour pro-
> ceedeth, should be altogether at his own will and plea-
> sure. . . . For it is no abatement of the *high Sovereignty* of
> the Glorious *God* over the world, that all his government
> and executing judgment, is ordered according to the natural
> and eternal rules and measures of *goodness* and *justice* and
> not by any such arbitrary will, which excludeth all respect
> thereto. And *man* hath not a less but a greater government
> over himself by the rules of *reason;* nor is it therefore any
> diminution of the power of a *Governour,* when the exercise
> thereof is and ought to be managed by the rules of *common*
> equity.[23]

In light of this more nuanced understanding of what was
involved in this "political theory of order" or "cosmic harmony," Daly, while endorsing Greenleaf's claim that it was
affiliated with the macrocosmic vision of the great chain of
being, is led to challenge the latter's further conclusion that
the theory justified support for "arbitrary and absolute monarchy," that it amounted to the theory of "the divine right of
kings typically defended by Sir Robert Filmer," that according to its terms "all limitations on the ruler, since they could
not be enforced on him, were merely moral, not 'practical or
politically important.'"[24]

"Absolute," Daly points out, was a term that in the early
seventeenth century possessed a wide spectrum of meanings,

not all of them political and most possessed of favorable connotations. Thus, for example, it was used in general as a synonym for "pure" or as suggestive of completeness or perfection (as in the case of God), and, in a political context, for example, to denote the perfection of a ruler's title (i.e., his independence of any foreign or external power), or, again, in a legal context, to denote "unconditional discretion" in relation to some particular sphere. This last strand of meaning points in the direction of the more negative connotations that were certainly present early in the century but that came to dominate only in the wake of the Civil Wars, when absolute rulership did indeed come generally to be taken to imply the arbitrary and unlimited. Filmer, admittedly, explicitly embraced that equation, but this very fact makes him a poor guide to the understanding of the term widespread among earlier thinkers, for Filmer, *pace* Greenleaf, was in this "unique among royalists."[25] That equation, indeed, is wholly "at variance with cosmic harmony, with its horror of will, its belief in indwelling law," its emphasis on cooperation, balance, limit, restraint. Restraint in response to the promptings of an immanent moral order and self-imposed, no doubt. But no weaker for that. It is really improper to appeal to Hobbes to support the contention that self-limitation is no limitation at all. For Hobbes's system, nominalist and voluntarist to the core, "is about as remote as it is possible to get intellectually from the mind of cosmic harmony."[26]

What is involved here is not exactly a standoff. Daly's evocation of the vision of cosmic harmony, and especially his stress on the priority it accorded to the rational principle in man as well as God, on its "horror of will," on its conviction that human society, like the cosmos itself, was permeated by an immanent, indwelling order—all of these emphases comport with the world view expressed in Lovejoy's great chain of being with a faithfulness and degree of precision to which

Greenleaf does not quite attain. But for anyone who has endured the long march down through the centuries from Jerome's letter to Eustochium and Damiani's argument at Monte Cassino, there is something a little troubling both about one or two of the things Daly mentions and about some on which he is well-nigh silent. Thus, to illustrate the former, it is odd that when he cites Richard Hooker's rejection of Puritan suggestions that "of the will of God to do this or that there is no reason besides his will," he quotes Hooker's comment that God's omnipotence is not qualified by the law that governs his actions "because the imposition of this law upon himself is his own free and voluntary act"[27]—a statement that comports ill with his own proper stress on the rationalism of the cosmic harmonists, whereas Hooker's earlier insistence that the law he has in mind is nothing other than the unchangeable "counsel of God" and that "the being of God is a kind of law to his working"[28] (in effect, Aquinas Englished) resonates much more faithfully to that frequency. And, to illustrate the latter, it is odd that he makes such selective use of James I's 1609 speech to Parliament, the more so in that Filmer, in stressing the superiority of king to law, seeks to wrap James I's mantle around him by citing from his *Trew Law of Free Monarchies* sentiments that find even clearer expression in that speech.[29] To that speech and those sentiments, then, it behoves us to return.

III

When we left James dangling, he was making of his subjects "like men at the Chesse; A pawne to take a Bishop or a Knight, and to cry up, or downe to any of their subjects, as they do their money." Almost immediately thereafter, however, he went on:

But now in these our times we are to distinguish betweene
the state of Kings in their first originall, and betweene the
state of setled Kings and Monarches, that doe at this time
governe in civill Kingdomes: For even as God, during the
time of the olde Testament, spake by Oracles, and wrought
by Miracles; yet how soone it pleased him to setle a *Church*
which was bought, and redeemed by the blood of his onely
Sonne *Christ*, then was there a cessation of both; Hee ever
after governing his people and Church within the limits of
his reveiled will. So in the first originall of Kings, whereof
some had their beginning by Conquest, and some by election
of the people, their wills at that time served for Law; Yet
how soone Kingdomes began to be setled in civilitie and
policie, then did Kings set downe their minds by Lawes,
which are properly made by the King onely; but at the roga-
tion of the people, the Kings grant being obteined thereunto.
And so the King became to be *Lex loquens*, after a sort,
binding himselfe by a double oath to the observation of the
fundamentall Lawes of his Kingdome. . . . So as every just
King in a setled Kingdome is bound to observe that paction
made to his people by his Lawes, in framing his government
agreeable thereunto, according to that paction which God
made witn *Noe* after the deluge. . . . And therefore a King
governing in a setled Kingdome, leaves off to be a King and
degenerates into a Tyrant, as soone as he leaves off to rule
according to his Lawes. . . . For it is a great difference betweene a Kings government in a setled State, and what Kings
in their originall power might doe in *Individuo vago*. . . . I
conclude then this point touching the power of Kings, with
this Axiome of Divinitie, That as to dispute what God may
doe, is Blasphemie; but *quid vult Deus*, that Divines may
lawfully, and doe ordinarily dispute and discusse; for to dispute *A Posse ad Esse* is both against Logicke and Divinitie:
So it is sedition in Subjects, to dispute what a King may do in
the height of his power: But just kings wil ever be willing to
declare what they wil do, if they wil not incurre the curse of
God. I wil not be content that my power be disputed upon:
but I shall ever be willing to make the reason appeare of all
my doings, and rule my actions according to my Lawes.[30]

Side by side with these words should be placed a similar
passage in a speech he delivered some six years later:

That which concernes the mysterie of the Kings power is not lawfull to be disputed; for that is to wade into the weaknesse of Princes, and to take away the mysticall reverence, that belongs unto them that sit in the Throne of God. . . . Keepe you therefore all in your owne bounds, and for my part, I desire you to give me no more right in my private Prerogative, than you give to any Subject; and therein will I be acquiescent: As for the absolute Prerogative of the Crowne, that is no Subject for the tongue of a lawyer, nor is it lawfull to be disputed.

It is Atheisme and blasphemie to dispute what God can doe: good Christians content themselves with his will revealed in his word. So, it is presumption and high contempt in a Subject, to dispute what a King can doe, or say that a King cannot doe this, or that; but rest in that which is the Kings revealed will in his Law.[31]

Now these are complex passages and I will need to recur to them yet once more before we finish. But for the time being, let me simply advance the claim that what James is busy doing here is distinguishing between the absolute and ordinary powers of the king. I advance that claim with great confidence, even though here he himself does not quite use those terms, because he comes even closer to doing so elsewhere.[32] So, too, do other early-modern English authors, and they do so, in fact, repeatedly. Thus one could cite references to the distinction ranging from one in the Year Book for 1469—during the reign, that is, of Edward IV—being applied there, however, to the difference between the legal powers wielded by the Court of Chancery and those wielded by the common law courts, to references in a report sent to his superiors in 1551 by Daniel Barbaro, the Venetian ambassador, in theoretical works written by such common lawyers as William Lambarde and Sir John Doddridge at the end of that century, or, in the seventeenth century, by such professors of civil law as John Cowell and Albericus Gentilis, or by such other authors as Edward Forset (whom both Greenleaf and Daly cite) and Sir John Davies, attorney general for

Ireland. References occur also in the political writings of Sir
Francis Bacon, in the acts of the Privy Council, in the records
of parliamentary debates, and in the judgments handed down
by the royal lawyers in several of the great Stuart state trials
concerning the reach of the royal prerogative—most notably
in that delivered by Chief Baron (i.e., Chief Judge) Fleming in
the Court of Exchequer in Bate's Case (1606) concerning the
king's power to impose without recourse to Parliament additional duties on imports.[33]

If Daly refers only glancingly to all of this and Greenleaf
not at all,[34] we should be appropriately understanding. The
texts in question, emanating from such various quarters—
political, publicistic, legal (and two different legal traditions
at that)—pose truly formidable problems of interpretation,
and the distinguishing feature of much of the scholarly comment has been its vagueness.[35] "Absolute" and "ordinary" as
used by sixteenth-and seventeenth-century lawyers were, we
are told, "unresolved terms."[36] Their use by Fleming was
"mysterious."[37] His judgment was "a fumbling and tenta-
tive expression of a quite indefinite theory,"[38] and "difficult
to understand . . . as an exposition of law."[39] And even
where it has not been vague, scholarly opinion has been divided. Thus William Holdsworth, the historian of English
law, believed the Stuart distinction between the absolute and
ordinary powers of the king to have resulted from the trans-
position by Tudor lawyers into a new key of the cognate
distinction used in the fifteenth century to denote the disparate legal powers wielded by the Court of Chancery and the
common law courts. But whereas the Tudor lawyers had
used it to discriminate between "the doing of such acts, as to
which he [the king] had [by custom] an unfettered discretion,
and the doing of such acts, such as the issue of proclama-
tions, the making of grants, or the seizure of property for
which the law had prescribed conditions," under James I it
began to be taken to suggest that of his absolute power the
king "was freed generally from legal restraint" and had "an

overriding absolute prerogative to deal with matters of state."[40]

Charles Howard McIlwain thought otherwise. Bolder and less insular in his approach, he saw the distinction as "about the same" as the one that he thought the thirteenth-century English jurist Henry of Bracton had drawn between *gubernaculum* and *jurisdictio*, "government" and "jurisdiction." And that distinction of Bracton's he regarded as "nothing but a commonplace of late-thirteenth century European political theory," indeed, as lying at the very heart of medieval constitutionalism. By *gubernaculum*, according to McIlwain, Bracton meant the government of the kingdom, which pertained to the king alone and in which there was no limit to his discretion. This was the realm of the later absolute power. By *jurisdictio*, on the other hand, he meant "those prescriptive rights of tenants or subjects which are wholly outside and beyond the legitimate bounds of the royal administration." This was the realm of the later ordinary power. The king swore to maintain those rights and they formed "a negative, legal limit" to his government.

What was involved, then, was a constitutional ideal that postulated a "parallelism" between government and jurisdiction, not the hierarchical subordination of one to the other, a monarchy, that is, that was absolute, but absolute only "within certain definite legal limits established by law." And what happened during the constitutional crisis in seventeenth-century England was that that parallelism broke down. The king, on the one side, began to extend his discretionary claims and to assert the superiority of his absolute power over the ordinary. Galvanized thereby into resistance, his legal and parliamentary critics, on the other, did the reverse, and began to rely exclusively "on the precedents of the ancient *jurisdictio*" and to try to impose a "new and unprecedented" legal and political control over the absolute power.[41]

This whole sweeping case, amounting to nothing less

than an overall interpretation of medieval constitutionalism
and of the reasons for its breakdown, McIlwain argued brilliantly in his book *Constitutionalism: Ancient and Modern.*
And since its publication in 1940, discussion of the issue has
proceeded in large part in his terms and within the framework of his theory.[42] But, of course, so far as the distinction
between the absolute and ordinary powers of the king is concerned, it just won't do. And not simply because Bractonian
scholars are now claiming that "the distinction between *jurisdictio* and *gubernaculum* . . . seems the product of McIlwain's classificatory acumen rather than Bracton's."[43] No
one, surely, who is aware of the long history of the parallel
theological distinction between the absolute and ordained
powers of God can rest content without broadening the context of the discussion and bringing this particular issue in the
history of legal and political thought into contact with the
larger history of the covenantal theme that we have been
exploring. The less so, indeed, in that Bible scholars now
assure us that the link between the two is present already in
the text of the Bible itself. For it has been argued, and on very
compelling grounds, that Israel took a political model to describe Yahweh's pact with her and her own peculiarly covenantal relationship with him, namely, the ancient Near East-
ern treaty form, especially that very one-sided form whereby
a powerful suzerain conceded his terms and freely pledged
his loyalty to a faithful vassal.[44] The less so, too, in that,
distinguishing between the powers of God, many a medieval
author—Aegidius Romanus, Duns Scotus, William of
Ockham, Pierre d'Ailly, John Major—attempted to illumi-
nate the theological distinction by referring to royal or papal
analogies.[45] The less so, again, in that among the seventeenth-century scientists who sounded the covenantal
theme, Descartes and Walter Charleton drew similar analogies.[46] The less so, finally, when one actually scrutinizes the
pertinent texts in the works of such men as Sir John Davies

and Edward Forset—the latter the author whom Daly clearly regards as the true virtuoso, the lead singer, as it were, among the cosmic harmonists.

Thus Davies tells us that "by the positive law the King himself was pleased to limit and stint his absolute power, and to tye himself to the ordinary rules of the law, in common and ordinary cases," but that he retained and reserved "notwithstanding in many points that absolute and unlimited power which was given unto him by the Law of Nations." And in this "he doth imitate the Divine Majesty, which in the Government of the world doth suffer things for the most part to passe according to the order and course of Nature, yet many times doth shew his extraordinary power in working of miracles above Nature.[47] And Forset: "For as we rightly conceive of God, that albeit he worketh efficiently, and (if I may so say) *naturally*, by the mediate causes, yet his potencie is not so by them tied or confined, but that he often performeth his owne pleasure by *extraordinarie* meanes, drawne out of his absolute power, both *praeter et contra naturam*. . . . To this likenesse of God . . . let us also shape our [regal] Sovereigntie."[48]

What, then, do we find if we do enlarge the context of the discussion? We find that from the late thirteenth century onward, side by side with the theological tradition of distinguishing between the absolute and ordained powers of God and touching it at more than one point ran a parallel tradition of distinguishing between the absolute and ordained or ordinary or civil or regulated powers (the latter terms tend to be used interchangeably) of popes, emperors, and kings. The kings of France and Hungary, it should be noted, as well as the English monarchs. Thus, among the civil lawyers who spoke severally of the German emperors and the French and English kings, the litany of those invoking the distinction runs from Baldus de Ubaldis in the fourteenth century, via Innocent Gentillet, Barthelémy Chasseneux and Jean Bodin in the sixteenth, to William Barclay, Albericus Gentilis, and John Cowell in the seventeenth.[49] In support of his own use of the distinction Bodin cited the authority of Pope Innocent IV, one of the most distinguished of medieval canon lawyers. Though I have not found the precise terms "absolute" and "ordinary" in Innocent, the notion is certainly there,[50] and other canonists of the thirteenth and fourteenth centuries, such as Hostiensis and Johannes Andreae, were quite explicit on the matter.[51] And if one steps outside the ranks of the professional lawyers, one finds the distinction invoked in a range of documents variegated enough in provenance and type to suggest that its use was not uncommon.[52]

Now in this distinction between the two powers of the pope, both Hostiensis and Johannes Andreae invoke the divine parallel, Hostiensis mentioning also Jerome's views on the sad case of the fallen virgin, which Gratian in the twelfth century had incorporated into his *Decretum*, later to become the textbook on which countless generations of aspiring canonists were to cut their juristic teeth.[53] And in his *De ecclesiastica potestate*, Aegidius Romanus—no canonist admittedly, but theologian and publicist—elaborates the parallelism at great length. Although by his absolute power, he says, the pope is "without halter and bit," nevertheless he himself ought to regulate his own actions. Thus, though he is above all positive laws, it is fitting that he should govern the church by his "regulated power," that is, in accordance with "the common law," taking in this regard "an example from God himself, whose vicar he is."[54] For God does not normally interfere with the operation of the secondary causes, which reflect, after all, the laws that he himself has given to nature. In God and the pope, however, there resides a plenitude of power by which they can do directly, without the intermediary of secondary causality, whatsoever they can do indirectly by means of them. Thus, for some special reason, God can act "aside from"

(*praeter*) the common laws of nature and perform a miracle—
as he did in Nebuchadnezzar's fiery furnace. Similarly, for
some comparably special reason, the pope can act "aside
from" the laws of the church and himself perform a function
that is commonly the task of a secondary agent. In other
words, though Aegidius does not quite say so, the pope, by an
exercise of his absolute power, can perform a papal miracle.[55]

Here as elsewhere, no less in seventeenth-century England than earlier on, the invocation of the divine analogy
underlines the fact that there is no question of the distinction's simply denoting the sort of parallelism that McIlwain
had in mind. Nor, clearly, was the assertion of the superiority
of the absolute power to the ordained or ordinary, as Holdsworth suggested, a contribution of the Stuart lawyers under
the novel political and constitutional conditions of seventeenth-century England.

Two things, however, should be noted. First: a point directed against Greenleaf's assumption that the argument
from the divine correspondence served solely to bolster royal
absolutism. When applied to popes, emperors, and kings, the
distinction also implied limits, self-imposed no doubt but
real enough for those who wished, for instance, to limit bur-
densome papal fiscal demands by evoking it *against* the
pope.[56] Second: a point directed against Daly's reluctance to
concede that effective limits to a ruler's power could be conceived as grounded not in the very nature of things but in the
ruler's own will. It should not be overlooked that one such
opposition group, while appealing to the pope's "ordained"
or "regulated" power, in order to stress the limits within
which he should ordinarily operate, underlined the self-imposed nature of the limits they had in mind by conceding
nonetheless that "by his plenitude of power (which power is
infinite) the same lord our pope can act above and against the
law, especially those laws which are of positive justice, and
can dispense and derogate from them or abrogate them."[57]

Although this assertion involves a negative assessment of
the normal range of papal power, not even Aegidius Romanus
himself conceived the absolute power of the pope in more
far-reaching terms.

What leads both Greenleaf and Daly astray on this matter,
though in differing ways, is their failure to perceive that confusingly intermingled in the divine correspondences that
their seventeenth-century English authors evoke are parallelisms of differing and ultimately incompatible types, comprehensible only in terms of radically different understandings of the nature of God and his relation to the universe. The
first are those parallelisms that Greenleaf and Daly have ex-
plicated so very well, namely, those that make sense in terms
of that philosophy of order or cosmic harmony which was the
reflection in the realm of political thinking of the complex
Greek understanding of the divine and its relation to the
universe summed up in the notion of the great chain of being.
The second are those parallelisms that they miss, namely,
those that make sense only when seen to refer to the biblical
God of might and power, who of his incomprehensible goodness and mercy has condescended in his governance of the
world and of men freely to bind himself to sustain the order
indicated in his covenant, pact, or promise. Daly's manifest
uneasiness about the notion of sovereign will—even when it
is echoed in the texts he cites—springs, I believe, from his
assumption that if one concedes such an untrammeled sovereign will, one has to relinquish the security of a stable
order. In this his instincts are similar to those of many a
disapproving commentator on the late-medieval theological
or seventeenth-century scientific use of the distinction between the divine powers.[58] But, as we have seen, such instincts contrive to mislead. The choice, it must once more be
insisted, is not one between order and sovereign will, *but one
between two different conceptions of order.* The one, order as
immanent, grounded in the very natures or essences of

things, is clearly incompatible with the notion of sovereign will. The other, order as external to things, imposed, as it were, from the outside, presupposes that very notion of sovereign will, presupposes that it would be contradictory to suggest that omnipotent will could not itself bind omnipotent will, presupposes the conviction that that will has stooped so to bind itself.

Of course, having said all of this, I must hastily concede that when the notions of omnipotence and covenant were invoked in the legal or political sphere, they were invoked only by analogy, and that the sharp edges of the distinction between the absolute and ordinary powers tended to be blunted when it descended from the purity of the theological empyrean and plunged into the density of the juristic atmosphere. The absolute power of God, curtailed only by the principle of noncontradiction, transcended all laws, physical, natural, divine. The absolute power of the pope, however, was conceived usually to transcend only the human positive law, not the natural or divine. Similarly the absolute power of the prince, which in the eyes of most civil lawyers was inferior also to the binding force of contracts made with his subjects. The complexity and tenacity of the native legal traditions that the distinction had to pierce as it made its way along the trajectory of the Roman law into French and English juristic thinking did something to further that process of modification, so much so, indeed, that under the impact of notions of fundamental law or of common law, there are occasions on which the outlines of the distinction became blurred and the precise meaning accorded to it hard to grasp.[59]

The rhetoric of their overeager propagandists to the contrary, moreover, popes, emperors, and kings were not God, and thinkers willing to repose their confidence in the reliability of God's covenant or promise were not necessarily as eager to repose the same sort of confidence in a human ruler's freely willed self-limitation. Thus, in the late thirteenth century, the theologian Henry of Ghent, while conceding that the pope did indeed possess a valid absolute power capable of transcending the legal dispositions in terms of which he governed *de potentia ordinata*, judged the actual exercise of such an absolute power nonetheless to be sinful "because it harmed the community's well-being by violating its fundamental laws."[60] In the sixteenth century, similar worries led the French Huguenot Lambert Daneau simply to reject the distinction, and Rycharde Taverner, one of Thomas Cromwell's men, to write with sorrow about those who invoked it: "wolde God the eares of chrystian rulers were not tykled with lyke tales, and yf they be that they wold with lyke severitie reject them."[61]

Because of these complexities (and others of more practical nature, too) I would not wish to be taken as suggesting that the covenantal tradition should constitute the sole intellectual context or can provide the master key for interpreting especially the diverse array of seventeenth-century English texts in which the distinction between the two powers is evoked. What I *am* suggesting is that it must be part of that context, provide one of the bunch of interpretive keys with which we seek to unlock the meaning of those frequently baffling texts. And to illustrate the value of that particular key I propose to return once more and by way of conclusion to the passages from two of James I's speeches cited earlier.

A reading of those texts with the covenantal theme in mind will suggest, I believe, that in them—and especially in the speech of 1609—James I intended to make gestures more conciliatory and claims less absolutistic than has usually been taken to be the case. The more so in that he blends the distinction between the absolute and ordinary powers with another even older and somewhat narrower theological distinction that had enjoyed a continuous life from the time of Hugh of St. Victor in the twelfth century down well into the seventeenth century—occurring for example, in Lombard's *Sentences* and in the works of Aquinas, Ockham, Luther, Ames, Charleton, and Hobbes.⁶² It was the distinction between the *voluntas dei beneplaciti,* variously referred to as the will of God's good pleasure or his concealed, secret, or hidden will, and the *voluntas dei signi,* commonly referred to as his "signifying" or "revealed" will—signified or revealed, that is, in "the word of God contained in the holy Scriptures."⁶³

In the years immediately before James I's 1609 address there had appeared several editions of the collected works of William Perkins, distinguished Puritan theologian and influential teacher at the Cambridge of the late sixteenth century. And in the *Treatise of God's Free Grace and Man's Free-will,* reprinted therein, the following passage occurs:

> This [divine] will is one and the same, as God is one: yet may it be distinguished in this manner. It is either *the will of his good pleasure,* or *his signifying will.* The truth of this distinction we may see in earthly Princes, who beare the image of God. A King determines within himselfe according to his pleasure what shall be done in his kingdome, and what not: this is his will. Againe, he signifies some part of his secret pleasure to his subjects, as occasion shall be offered, and this is also his wil. Even so the pleasure of GOD within himselfe, and the significations thereof to his creature either in whole or in part, are his will.⁶⁴

No more than in the case of that other distinction between the absolute and ordinary powers, then, was there anything unprecedented about James I's application of this distinction to his own royal power. Thus, in these texts, the king's absolute power or prerogative—which refers to what he *can* do— is further identified as that power which is mysterious, unlimited, and "not lawfull to be disputed." Similarly, his "private prerogative" (i.e., ordinary power)—which operates

within the limits of the established laws—is identified instead as a power clearly fit for discussion, for it is "the king's
revealed will in his Law." At the same time, these identifica-
tions are buttressed with further correspondences on the divine level. Just as it is blasphemous "to dispute what God
can doe" of his absolute power, *"quid vult Deus,* that Divines may lawfully, and doe ordinarily dispute and discusse"—for what is involved here is the "revealed will" of
God, within the limits of which he normally operates and
which is "revealed in his word."[65]

It should be noted that the distinction between the hidden and revealed wills was somewhat narrower in scope than
that between the absolute and ordinary powers. In theology it
was used characteristically to refer not to the activity of the
divine will in general but rather to that activity in so far as it
pertained to the moral order or the economy of salvation.
Thus the *voluntas beneplaciti* is the direct will of God,
which is always implemented. Being God's eternal counsel,
it is of its nature to be hidden or concealed from man. The
voluntas signi, on the other hand, is "the declaration or revelation of God's will for his creation which enables man to
know the will of God." That is to say, it is the law, and, as
such, "it is certainly not always executed."[66] And the intent
of the distinction is to stress the fact that the vital thing for
man is to eschew futile speculation about the disposition of
God's hidden will and to acquaint himself, instead, with that
revealed will whereby God makes known to man the divine
modus operandi in the moral sphere and in the economy of
salvation.[67]

The nature of this intent comes out very clearly in one of
the treatises on free will written in 1527 by the Swiss Anabaptist Balthasar Hübmaier. The passage is of particular interest to us in that Hübmaier, like James I later on, blends the
distinction between the hidden and revealed wills with that
between the absolute and ordinary powers. Thus he contrasts

God's "omnipotent and hidden will" (*voluntas absoluta*), by which he "has full right and power to do with us whatever he will" and by which he can be said to harden the hearts of the damned, with his "revealed" or "ordinary" will, in accordance with which he "does not want to harden, to blind, to damn anyone, save those who of their own evil and by their own choice wish to be hardened, blinded, and damned." It is this latter will that we encounter in God's "preached and revealed Word," and from it we learn that "although God is omnipotent, and can do all things, yet he will not act toward us poor human beings according to his omnipotence, but according to his mercy, as he amply proved to us by his most beloved Son." The secret will of God is to be left, then, "in its worthy majesty, as something we have no need to investigate." It is with the revealed will that we should concern ourselves, and it is a will that assures our moral freedom.[68]

The similarity in intent of James I's use of these distinctions is striking. If the "absolute prerogative" of the crown is a mystery that is not to be disputed, subjects may quite properly concern themselves with that other will which the king has "declared" and "revealed" in his law. Indeed, they should concern themselves with that revealed will, for, if it does not indicate what the king of his absoluteness *can* do, it does declare what he *will* do. And as James after all insists: "I shall ever be willing to rule my actions according to my Lawes."

Doubtless, the conciliatory nature of these sentiments was concealed from his audience of parliamentarians and common lawyers by the fact that James, faithful both to the theological parallels he was invoking and to his own Scottish heritage of Roman law, claimed that the laws were *his* laws, a revelation merely of *his* will.[69] But it is underlined by the further restriction on his power which he willingly concedes when he contrasts the free and miraculous divine activity evident "during the time of the Olde Testament" with God's

willingness after the Incarnation to govern "his people and
Church within the limits of his reveiled will."[70] For he goes
on to draw a parallel with the similar contrast "between the
state of Kings in their originall" and "the state of setled
Kings and Monarches, that doe at this time governe in civill
Kingdomes." If in the former the royal will itself could serve
directly for law, in the latter "Kings set down their minds by
lawes" and bound themselves "to observe that paction" and
to rule in accordance with those laws. This contrast, James
insists, is not to be slighted. The failure of one of the previous
speakers before the assembled houses to draw attention to it
was precisely the point that led him "by divers" to be "mistaken or not wel understood." "For what he spake of a Kings
power in *Abstracto*, is most trew in Divinitie." It was simply
that he did not make the necessary distinction "betweene
the generall power of a King in Divinity, and the settled and
established State of this Crowne, and Kingdome."[71]

While it would, of course, be improper to make too much
of James I's precision or clarity in these central theoretical
statements of his, it would equally be improper, as was long
the practice, to make too little of it. These statements are
unlikely to be understood at all unless, as Greenleaf has insisted, we take the argument by correspondence as seriously
as it was intended. And they are likely to be understood
inadequately, I now add, unless it is recognized that when (in
these passages at least) James invokes his battery of divine
correspondences, what he is doing is not striking any chords
reminiscent of Daly's cosmic harmony or evocative of Lovejoy's great chain of being but rather deploying two well-worn
scholastic distinctions that lie at the heart of the covenantal
tradition. And what that recognition suggests is the interesting likelihood that it was his intention by so doing to soften
for his audience the somewhat uncompromising contours of
an otherwise distressingly absolutistic effusion.

EPILOGUE

At the start of this discussion I set myself two tasks. First, to trace from the twelfth to the seventeenth centuries the history of the theme on which pivoted, during those centuries, a coherent scheme of things contrasting sharply with the picture evoked by the notion of the great chain of being but rivaling it by its own imaginative force. That theme: the distinction between the absolute and ordained or ordinary powers. That scheme: the vision of an order—natural, moral, salvational, political—grounded not in the very nature of things but rather in will, promise, and covenant. By reconstructing that history I intended, and in the second place, to suggest that Lovejoy's approach to the history of ideas can properly lay a much greater claim to our respect than most historians seem currently willing to concede.

In relation to the first of those tasks, and resisting now

the temptation to pursue the echoes and harmonics of the covenantal tradition on into the intricate histories of legal positivism or the emergence of political theories of legitimation by consent,[1] I have little further to add. While the covenantal tradition certainly persisted beyond the opening years of the eighteenth century, the distinction between the absolute and ordained powers appears to have faded into oblivion. In relation to the second task, however, some additional comment may be appropriate.

Having begun by rejecting in principle the charge that Lovejoy's approach to the history of ideas is "wrong in principle" and having striven in practice to prove mistaken the claim that histories written in accord with the canons of that approach "can never go right," I have now simply to indicate wherein I believe its particular value to reside. Not, clearly, as the sole—perhaps not even as the primary—approach to intellectual history. Even if its scope were not too narrow to encompass the broad range of concerns intellectual historians have properly made their own, the very degree of its dependence on the labors of those working in other branches of the history of thought should suffice to inhibit, even in the boldest of its practitioners, any aspirations either monopolistic or hegemonic. That dependence Lovejoy himself of course acknowledged as inevitable in an enterprise committed to the hot pursuit of ideas across the borders—national, chronological, linguistic, disciplinary—that academic specialization has conspired to endorse and academic training contrived, willy-nilly, to perpetuate.[2] And of late it has even been claimed that "the history of an idea, basically, is a second order enquiry which is to a large extent *parasitic* on the detailed historical study of individual authors."[3]

To the extent to which that charge is true, the Lovejovian historian of ideas, as he cuts a swathe across whole series of intensely cultivated scholarly specialties, is likely in unusual degree to be error-prone, burdened by responsibility for a very disparate array of texts, peculiarly susceptible to misreading the intricate scholarly controversies that trouble practically every field, an exposed (if moving) target drawing the irritated fire of successive platoons of specialists jealously guarding the confines of their own well-fortified enclaves.[4] So much so, indeed, that the whole enterprise would be a great deal harder to justify did it not serve to expose another range of errors, no less deleterious to accurate historical understanding but much less frequently celebrated by the critics; namely, the type of misreading (as with the late-medieval nominalists, or with Robert Boyle, or James I) into which the more time-bound specialists are sometimes betrayed by framing too narrowly the context in which they struggle to wrest an authentically historical meaning from their texts. For the context in which a text is to be understood is no more a simple given than is the meaning we ascribe to that text.[5] It is the product, rather, of historical reconstruction. As such it inevitably reflects the interpretive choice of the historian, and it is one of the great strengths of Lovejoy's approach to the history of ideas that it adopts an interpretive strategy in the absence of which some texts—notably those embodying the more migratory of ideas—are doomed to be improperly or inadequately understood.

It does so, as we have seen, by taking as its subject matter a certain type of intellectual tradition. Not, admittedly, the sort of tradition classically identified by Michael Oakeshott when he schematized the history of political thought in accordance with the "master-conceptions" of reason and nature, will and artifice, and the rational will. Wonderfully illuminating though those schemata can be, rather than embodying identifiably *historical* traditions they appear to reflect the historian's own organizing or analytic principles.[6] Nor, again, traditions merely "of argument or discourse"—I use that term now to denote those traditions "which centre on a related set of questions or common concerns"—but

rather full-blown "traditions of thought," which, in responding to such questions and concerns, embody also shared con-
stellation of "beliefs and values."[7] Such traditions, by no
means static or unchanging but preserving across time a certain continuity, identity, and authority, not only constitute
intelligible and viable subjects of historical investigation but
also, it has plausibly been argued, provide "an appropriate
framework for understanding linguistic performances (words
and texts)."[8]

If, then, one is prepared to conclude with Collingwood
that in order to lay firm hold on a past writer's purpose[9] one
must identify the question he was trying to answer, the problem he was trying to solve, one would do well to concede also
(and especially if the author involved is a scholastic) that that
question along with its presuppositions is likely to be a historical deliverance, and that the author's particular intellectual inheritance must necessarily constitute a crucial part of
his "problem situation," of the contemporaneous context
that holds the key to his intended meaning. Even if one ig-
nores the institutional or general cultural mediation of that
inheritance, books after all play an enormously important
role in the lives of intellectuals—conveying memories of a
very distant past, posing questions sometimes of very ancient provenance, mediating ideas whose "particular go" has
survived intact the hostility of time and is capable still of
launching thoughts into sometimes unexpected orbits. To
have given so very powerful a recognition to that fact was
perhaps the greatest of Lovejoy's achievements. And what
better a way to reaffirm that recognition than to celebrate his
achievement?

Notes

1. Against the Stream: In Praise of Lovejoy

1. I have drawn most of my information on these matters from the following assessments of the development of historical studies since World War II: "New Ways of History," *Times Literary Supplement,* April 7, July 28, September 8, 1966; "The Historian's Craft," ibid., March 7, 1975, 238–40, 246, 255–56; "New Trends in History," *Daedalus* 98 (Fall 1969): 888–96; Felix Gilbert and Stephen R. Graubard, eds., *Historical Studies Today* (New York, 1972); J. H. Hexter, "Fernand Braudel and the *Monde Braudelien* . . . ," *Journal of Modern History* 44, no. 4 (1972):480–539; Charles F. Delzell, ed., *The Future of History* (Nashville, Tenn., 1977); Georg G. Iggers and Harold T. Parker, eds., *International Handbook of Historical Studies: Contemporary Research and Theory* (Westport, Conn., 1979); Michael Kammen, ed., *The Past before Us: Contemporary Historical Writing in the United States* (Ithaca, 1980); Fernand Braudel, *On History*, trans. Sarah Matthews (Chicago, 1980); Lawrence Stone, *The Past and the Present* (Boston, 1981); Bernard Bailyn, "The Challenge of Modern Historiography," *American Historical Review* 87, no. 1 (1982):1–24. For analyses

in more prophetic mode, see the essays gathered together under the heading "The New History: The 1980s and Beyond," in *Journal of Interdisciplinary History* 12 nos. 1 and 2 (1981):1–332.

2. Michael Kammen, "The Historian's Vocation and the State of the Discipline in the United States," in *Past before Us*, ed. Kammen, 21.

3. Thus Edward Shils in the *Times Literary Supplement*, July 28, 1966, 647.

4. Stone, *Past and the Present*, 30.

5. Jacques Barzun, *Clio and the Doctors: Psycho-History, Quanto-History, and History* (Chicago, 1974); Gertrude Himmelfarb, "The 'New History,'" *Commentary* 59 (January 1975):72–78.

6. See, e.g., Gene Wise, "The Contemporary Crisis in Intellectual History Studies," *Clio* 5 (1975);55–72; Paul K. Conkin, "Intellectual History: Past, Present, and Future," in Delzell, *Future of History*, 111–27; Robert Darnton, "Intellectual and Cultural History," in *Past before Us*, ed. Kammen, 327–32; William J. Bouwsma, "From History of Ideas to History of Meaning," *Journal of Interdisciplinary History* 12 no. 2 (1981):279–89.

7. Dominick La Capra, as cited in Darnton, "Intellectual and Cultural History," 328.

8. Thus Conkin, "Intellectual History," 111, summing up "the pessimistic judgment, expressed in a number of recent obituaries" with which he disagrees. For a balanced assessment from a different national perspective, see Ernst Schulin, "Geistesgeschichte, Intellectual History, and Histoire des Mentalités seit der Jahrhundertwende," in his *Traditionskritik und Rekonstruktionsversuch* (Göttingen, 1979), 144–62.

9. The words are those of William Hesseltine, cited in Darnton, "Intellectual and Cultural History," 329.

10. See the statistics cited in ibid., 334–37.

11. Stone, *Past and the Present*, 43.

12. Ibid., 80–81, 83.

13. Ibid., 85–86.

14. Max Weber, "Gutachten zur Werturteilsdiskussion im Ausschuss des Vereins für Sozialpolitik," in Eduard Baumgarten, *Max Weber: Werk und Person* (Tübingen, 1964), 139. For commentary on this and other similar remarks by Weber, see the introduction by Guy Oakes to his translation of Max Weber, *Roscher and Knies: The Logical Problems of Historical Economics* (New York, 1975), 3–16.

15. Laurence Veysey, "The United States," in *International Handbook of Historical Studies*, ed. Iggers and Parker, 163.

16. The charge is levied by Benjamin I. Schwartz, "A Brief Defence of Political and Intellectual History with Particular Reference to Non-Western Cultures," in *Historical Studies Today*, ed. Gilbert and Graubard, 451.

17. Edith Kurzweil, *The Age of Structuralism: Lévi-Strauss to Foucault* (New York, 1980), presents in convenient form the pertinent biographical information and general historical background but is less than satisfactory in her analyses of theoretical positions. For these, reference may be made to Jonathan Culler, *Structuralist Poetics: Structuralism, Linguistics, and the Study of Literature* (Ithaca, 1975), and Christopher Norris, *Deconstruction: Theory and Practice* (New York, 1982). Two excellent collections of essays by prominent structuralists, poststructuralists, and fellow travelers are Richard Macksey and Eugenio Donato, eds., *The Structuralist Controversy: The Languages of Criticism and the Sciences of Man* (Baltimore, 1972), and Josué V. Harari, ed., *Textual Strategies: Perspectives in Post-Structuralist Criticism* (Ithaca, 1979).

18. Thus Sande Cohen, "Structuralism and the Writing of Intellectual History," *History and Theory* 17 (1978):175–206; Dominick La Capra, "Rethinking Intellectual History and Reading Texts," ibid., 19 (1980):245–76. See also La Capra, *Rethinking Intellectual History: Texts, Contexts, Language* (Ithaca, 1983), and E. M. Henning, "Archaeology, Deconstruction, and Intellectual History," in *Modern European Intellectual History*, ed. Dominick La Capra and Steven L. Kaplan (Ithaca, 1982), 153–96.

19. *Les Mots et les choses* (Paris, 1966), translated as *The Order of Things* (New York, 1970), 275; *L'Archéologie du savoir* (Paris, 1969), translated by A. M. Sheridan Smith as *The Archaeology of Knowledge* (New York, 1972), 138–39. It is the translations that I cite. I specify these works because it is here, rather than in Foucault's earlier writings, that the extent of his departure from the goals of the traditional historiography becomes evident. See Allan Megill, "Foucault, Structuralism, and the Ends of History," *Journal of Modern History* 51, no. 3 (1979):451–503; cf. G. S. Rousseau, "Whose Enlightenment? No Man's: The Case of Michel Foucault," *Eighteenth-Century Studies* 6, no. 2 (1972):239 and 256. My critical appraisal of these methodological words does not preclude an admiring recognition of the acuteness of some of Foucault's insights, especially those conveyed in his more recent explorations of the relationship between power and knowledge. For a helpful discussion and pertinent bibliography, see Alan Sheridan, *Foucault: The Will to Truth* (New York, 1980), 113–94.

20. Hayden White's phrase in "Foucault Decoded: Notes from Underground," *History and Theory* 12 (1973):27.

21. George Huppert, "*Divinatio et Eruditio*: Thoughts on Foucault," *History and Theory* 13 (1974):191–96. Cf. the dissent registered by Samuel Kinser, "*Annaliste* Paradigm?: The Geohistorical Structuralism of Fernand Braudel," *American Historical Review* 86, no. 1 (1981):64.

22. Foucault, *Order of Things*, 340–42. Foucault's affinity for Nietzsche is well discussed in Sheridan, *Michel Foucault*, esp. 113ff.

23. A point made with great clarity and persuasive power in Megill's fine article, "Foucault, Structuralism, and the Ends of History." See also White, "Foucault Decoded."

24. *Order of Things*, 17, 207, 308, 327.

25. Paul Veyne, *Comment on écrit l'histoire* (Paris, 1978), 203–4; cf. White, "Foucault Decoded," 49.

26. White, "Foucault Decoded," 26; Foucault, *Order of Things*, esp. 275–76.

27. White, "Foucault Decoded," 24–25. Cf. Schulin, *Traditionskritik*, 158–59; Megill, "Foucault, Structuralism and the Ends of History," esp. 493–94 (for "Foucault's final acknowledgment of his own lack of interest in the past") and 497 (for "his rejection of the conception of historical reality itself"); Michael S. Roth, "Foucault's 'History of the Present,'" *History and Theory* 20, no. 1 (1981):32–46.

28. For a helpful discussion of "perspectivism," see A. C. Danto, *Nietzsche as Philosopher* (New York, 1965), 68–99. Norris, *Deconstruction*, esp. 56–89, brings out very well the impact of Nietzsche's views on those of the deconstructionists.

29. J. P. Stern, *Friedrich Nietzsche* (Hammondsworth, 1978), 77, commenting on Nietzsche, *Will to Power*, §567.

30. See Michel Foucault, "What Is an Author?" in *Textual Strategies*, ed. Harari, 141–60; Roland Barthes, "From Work to Text," in ibid., 73–81.

31. Harold Bloom, "The Breaking of Form," in Harold Bloom et al., *Deconstruction and Criticism* (New York, 1979), 4; cf. Geoffrey Hartman's preface to the same volume, vii.

32. J. Hillis Miller, "The Critic as Host," in Bloom et al., *Deconstruction and Criticism*, 230; Foucault, *Order of Things*, xxiii and 382.

33. Barthes, "From Work to Text," in *Textual Strategies*, ed. Harari, 76–81.

34. M. H. Abrams, "How to Do Things with Texts," *Partisan Review* 46, no. 4 (1979): 568. The essay as a whole mounts a telling critique of the textual strategies proposed not only by Derrida but by two American "new readers" of less philosophical bent, Stanley Fish and Harold Bloom. Fish's reply in his *Is There a Text in This Class?: The Authority of Interpretative Communities* (Cambridge, Mass., 1980), 303–329, does not, I judge, succeed in deflecting the thrust of Abrams' criticism.

35. The words are those of Abrams, "How to Do Things with Texts," 581.

36. See especially the contributions of Bloom and Miller to Bloom et al., *Deconstruction and Criticism,* and the remarks of Gay Clifford, "The Benefits of Wilderness: Structuralist Criticism," *Encounter* 57 (July 1981):53–59.

37. E. D. Hirsch, Jr., *The Aims of Interpretation* (Chicago, 1976), 1. Cf. Hirsch, "The Politics of Theories of Interpretation," *Critical Inquiry* 9, no. 1 (1982):235–47, for a robust insistence on the centrality of historical interpretation as "the humanist pursuit par excellence" (246).

38. See Hirsch's comment (*Aims of Interpretation,* 91) on the displeasure of Barthes at having his intended meaning distorted by another scholar. Cf. Hirsch, "Politics of Theories of Interpretation," 240n5. Similarly Foucault. Karlis Racevskis, *Michel Foucault and the Subversion of Intellect* (Ithaca, 1983), 39, argues (somewhat paradoxically, it may be) that "to objectify Foucault by making him into the subject of his own discourse would amount to adopting a strategy of interpretation that Foucault specifically intends to discredit." But even if Foucault has indeed "frequently reiterated his wish to minimize his own authorial presence in his work as much as possible," his actions belie his theory. In a recent (and revealing) exchange with Lawrence Stone he rebukes the latter for having misread or misrepresented his line of argument in *Histoire de la folie à l'age classique.* "Don't you agree," he says, "that only by respecting the thought of an author can one prevent criticism from falling prey to the bad habits of hurried journalism?" See "An Exchange with Michel Foucault," in *New York Review of Books* 30, no. 5 (March 31, 1983):42.

39. It is perhaps fitting that Hayden V. White, who as long ago as 1969 drew attention to the importance of structuralism for historiography ("The Tasks of Intellectual History," *Monist* 52, no. 4 [1969]:606–30), should now sound a warning about the current "poststructuralist fetishization" of the "structuralist problematic." See "The Absurdist Movement in Contemporary Literary History," in White, *Tropics of Discourse: Essays in Cultural Criticism* (Baltimore, 1978), 361–82.

40. I borrow this arresting phrase from Edward W. Said, *Beginnings: Intention and Method* (New York, 1975), 338.

41. John Dunn, "The Identity of the History of Ideas," *Philosophy* 43 (April 1968):85–104; J. G. A. Pocock, *Politics, Language, and Time: Essays on Political Thought and History* (New York, 1971), 3–41; Quentin Skinner, "The Limits of Historical Explanations," *Philosophy* 41 (1966):199–215; "Meaning and Understanding in the History of Ideas," *History and Theory* 8 (1969):3–53; "Conventions and the Understanding of Speech Acts," *Philosophical Quarterly* 20 (1970):

118–38; "On Performing and Explaining Linguistic Actions," *Philo-sophical Quarterly* 21 (1971):1–21; "Motives, Intentions, and the In-terpretation of Texts," *New Literary History* 3, no. 2 (1972): 393–408; "Hermeneutics and the Role of History," *New Literary History* 7, no. 1 (1975):209–32; *The Foundations of Modern Political Thought,* 2 vols. (Cambridge, Eng., 1978), 1:ix–xv. Skinner's first two articles, in partic-ular, have elicited criticism. See, notably, Bhikhu Parekh and R. N. Berki, "The History of Political Ideas: A Critique of Q. Skinner's Meth-odology," *Journal of the History of Ideas* 34, no. 2 (1973):163–84; Charles Tarlton, "History, Meaning, and Revisionism in the Study of Political Thought," *History and Theory* 12 (1973)307–28 (criticizing also Pocock and Dunn); Gordon J. Schochet, "Political Thought and Political Action. A Symposium on Quentin Skinner: II. Quentin Skin-ner's Method," *Political Theory* 2, no. 3 (1974):261–76. Skinner mounts a carefully balanced reply to his critics in the third part of the same symposium—"Some Problems in the Analysis of Political Thought and Action," 277–303—but that has not deterred others from entering the lists. See John G. Gunnell, *Political Theory: Tradition and Interpretation* (Cambridge, Mass., 1979), 96–103, 119–20, where he also criticizes Pocock; cf. his subsequent exchange with Pocock in *Annals of Scholarship* 1, no. 4 (1980):3–62 (Pocock, "Political Theory, History, and Myth: A Salute to John Gunnell," 3–25; Gunnell, "Meth-od, Methodology, and the Search for Traditions in the History of Politi-cal Thought: A Reply to Pocock's Salute," 26–56; Pocock, "Intentions, Traditions, and Methods: Some Sounds on a Fog-Horn," 57–62). Also L. Mulligan, J. Richards, and J. Graham, "Intentions and Conventions: Quentin Skinner's Method for the Study of History of Ideas," *Political Studies* 27, no. 1 (1979):84–98; Andrew Lockyer, " 'Traditions' as Con-text in the History of Political Thought," *Political Studies* 27, no. 2 (1979):201–17; Joseph V. Femia, "An Historicist Critique of 'Revision-ist Methods for Studying the History of Ideas,' " *History and Theory* 20, no. 2 (1981):113–34.

42. Dunn, "Identity of the History of Ideas," 98.

43. Despite expressions of sympathy with the methodology pro-posed by Dunn and Skinner, Pocock is the least committed to this particular concern. See his *Politics, Language, and Time,* 6–7, 25, and, more strikingly, "Political Theory, History, and Myth," 13–14.

44. Skinner, "Meaning and Understanding," 49.

45. Skinner, "Some Problems," 283; "Motives, Intentions, and the Interpretation of Texts," 401–3. See also "Conventions and the Under-standing of Speech Acts," 118–38, for a fuller statement of the argument.

46. See, e.g., P. Mew, "Conventions on Thin Ice," *Philosophical Quarterly* 21 (October 1971):352–56, and the articles referred to above, n. 41.

47. Skinner, "Motives, Intentions, and the Interpretation of Texts," 404–5.

48. Skinner, "Some Problems," 287.

49. Skinner, "Meaning and Understanding," 3–53; cf. his subsequent comment: "Some Problems," 279.

50. Dunn, "Identity of the History of Ideas," 97.

51. Skinner, "Meaning and Understanding," 37.

52. Ibid., 35.

53. Skinner, "Some Problems," 279; cf. "Meaning and Understanding," 31.

54. Skinner, "Meaning and Understanding," 31.

55. Skinner, "Meaning and Understanding," 36 and 39.

56. John Passmore, "The Idea of a History of Philosophy," *History and Theory* 5 (1965):13.

57. See Arthur O. Lovejoy, *The Great Chain of Being: A Study of the History of an Idea* (Cambridge, Mass., 1936), 3–23; "The Historiography of Ideas," *Proceedings of the American Philosophical Society* 78, no. 4 (1938):529–43; "Reflections on the History of Ideas," *Journal of the History of Ideas* 1, no. 1 (1940):3–23; "The Meaning of Romanticism for the History of Ideas," *Journal of the History of Ideas* 2, no. 3 (1941):257–78; "Reply to Professor Spitzer," *Journal of the History of Ideas* 5, no. 2 (1944):204–19; *Essays in the History of Ideas* (Baltimore, 1948), xi–xv. Some illuminating comments on the "Lovejovian" methodology by close colleagues and collaborators may be found in the essays by George Boas, Maurice Mandelbaum, and Marjorie Nicolson contributed in honor of Lovejoy's seventy-fifth birthday to the *Journal of the History of Ideas* 9, no. 4 (1948):404–23, 428–38, in George Boas et al., *Studies in Intellectual History* (Baltimore, 1953), 3–21; in Philip P. Wiener, "Some Problems and Methods in the History of Ideas," *Journal of the History of Ideas* 22, no. 4 (1961):531–48; and in Maurice Mandelbaum, "The History of Ideas, Intellectual History, and the History of Philosophy," *History and Theory* 5 (1965):34–42. Edward P. Mahoney, "Metaphysical Foundations of the Hierarchy of Being According to Some Late-Medieval and Renaissance Philosophers," in *Philosophies of Existence: Ancient and Modern*, ed. Parviz Morewedge (New York, 1982), 165–257, provides among other things a valuable guide to the literature on the notion of the great chain of being that has appeared since the publication of Lovejoy's book. Skinner refers to the opening (methodological) chapter of *The Great Chain of Being* but

draws from Lovejoy's writings none of the errors he attributes to the practitioners of the traditional history of ideas. Other critics of that genre usually refer to Lovejoy's approach only in the most general terms and sometimes in such a fashion as to suggest that they could comfortably plead innocent to the charge of having read him. I find an apposite parallel in Felix Gilbert's comment on the present-day fate of Leopold von Ranke. Anyone who has read much of his work, he says,

> is simply unable to accept the view that Ranke was exclusively concerned with political and diplomatic history; he was much more aware of the issues of social and intellectual history than his critics allow. . . . Ranke's present critics are in revolt against the view of Ranke's principles as spread by his disciples rather than against those derived from a study of Ranke's works. But the frequency with which this misinterpretation occurs is characteristic and significant; it shows that Ranke is a name, a concept rather than a clearly seen personality. The conclusion is unavoidable: he is hardly read any longer." [*Historical Studies Today,* ed. Gilbert and Graubard, xv]

58. Lovejoy, "Reflections," 17.

59. Lovejoy, *Great Chain of Being,* 11.

60. He does not appear, for example, to have appraised very highly either the historical or the philosophical respectability of J. B. Bury's *Idea of Progress* (a work frequently adduced in the recent literature as an example of the traditional approach to the history of ideas). See Lovejoy, "Historiography of Ideas," 541–42.

61. Lovejoy, *Essays,* xiv.

62. Lovejoy, "Meaning of Romanticism," 259.

63. See Lovejoy, "On the Discrimination of Romanticisms," in *Essays in the History of Ideas,* 228–53; "The Thirteen Pragmatisms," in *The Thirteen Pragmatisms and Other Essays* (Baltimore, 1963), 1–29; and (with George Boas), *Primitivism and Related Ideas in Antiquity* (Baltimore, 1935), Appendix, 447–56.

64. Lovejoy, "Reflections," 9–16; cf. "Historiography of Ideas," 531–35.

65. Lovejoy, *Great Chain of Being,* 19–20; cf. "Historiography of Ideas," 533–55. George Boas comments that Lovejoy's earlier articles on the history of philosophy indicate "his profound sympathy with the less recognized genius," adding, "the history of philosophy thus becomes not the successive stories of a dozen outstanding figures, the Platos, Aristotles, and Kants, but rather the patient uncovering of hundreds of minor figures" ("A. O. Lovejoy as Historian of Philosophy," *Journal of the History of Ideas* 9, no. 4 [1948]:404–5). Cf. the similar

judgment by Marjorie Nicolson, "A. O. Lovejoy as Teacher," 435–36 of the same issue.

66. E.g., his insistence that what an author does *not* say is "of much more significance for the intellectual historian than is usually appreciated" ("Meaning of Romanticism," 264–65). (Cf. Skinner, "Meaning and Understanding," 47–48; *Foundations of Modern Political Thought,* 1:xiv). Or again, and more strikingly, his insistence in opposition to any crudely reductionist approach to the reading of texts as an "unmasking of ideologies" that

> once a rationalization has been formed, it is antecedently improbable—and could be shown by historical evidence to be untrue—that it will remain otiose and inert, having no repercussions upon the affective side of consciousness out of which it may have arisen. When a man has given a reason for his belief, his moral approbation or disapprobation, his aesthetic preference, he is—happily or otherwise—caught in a trap; for the reason is likely to entail, or seem to entail, consequences far beyond and, it may be, contrary to, the desire which generated it, or, not less awkwardly, contrary to undeniable matters of fact.   ["Reflections," 19]
> Cf. Skinner, "Some Problems," 294–95; *Foundations of Modern Political Thought,* 1:xii–xiii.

67. In discussing this approach to the reading of texts, Skinner frequently refers to the views of advocates of the "New Criticism" in literature. See "Meaning and Understanding," 3–4; "Motives, Intentions, and the Interpretation of Texts," 395–405; "Hermeneutics and the Role of History," 215–16.

68. Lovejoy, *Essays,* xii; "Reflections," 4; "Historiography of Ideas," 530–32.

69. Lovejoy, *Great Chain of Being,* 15; cf. "Historiography of Ideas," 532–35, where he sketches out the array of contextual information one should have at one's disposal fully to understand a mere two hundred lines in Milton's *Paradise Lost.*

70. Lovejoy, "Historiography of Ideas," 536–40; "Reflections," 6–9. Cf. his earlier urging of the need for collaborative inquiries in his presidential address to the American Philosophical Association, "On Some Conditions of Progress in Philosophical Inquiry," *Philosophical Review* 26, no. 2 (1917):123–63.

71. Lovejoy, *Great Chain of Being,* 3–7; "Historiography of Ideas," 537–39.

72. The above listing is a selective conflation of the similar but not identical listings Lovejoy gave in *Great Chain of Being,* 7–15, and "Historiography of Ideas," 538.

73. The book originated at Harvard in 1933 as the second series of the William James Lectures in Philosophy and Psychology, a series attended by a progressively dwindling audience that included few of Lovejoy's colleagues on the Harvard philosophy faculty. On the lectures and the place of his chosen topic in Lovejoy's thinking, see the recent biography by Daniel J. Wilson, *Arthur O. Lovejoy and the Quest for Intelligibility* (Chapel Hill, N.C., 1980), esp. 139–56, 186–91.
74. Lovejoy, *Great Chain of Being*, 31.
75. Ibid., 49.
76. Ibid., 58.
77. Ibid., 58–59.
78. Ibid.
79. Ibid., 61.
80. Ibid., 183.
81. Ibid., 245 and 259.
82. Ibid., 325–26.
83. Ibid., 3. Oddly enough, subsequent commentators have frequently missed the degree to which Lovejoy recognized the limitations inherent in his chosen approach. On this point William F. Bynum, "The Great Chain of Being after Forty Years: An Appraisal," *History of Science* 13 (1975):1, constitutes a happy exception. "[Lovejoy] saw," he says, "that there are various kinds of historical questions which could not be asked (much less answered) from his particular vantage point."
84. Lovejoy, "Reflections," 23.
85. For some interesting remarks on this aspect of "contextualism" (though not made with reference to Lovejoy), see La Capra, "Rethinking Intellectual History," 264. For some related reflections, see also Felix Gilbert, "Intellectual History: Its Aims and Methods," 144–45, and Thomas S. Kuhn, "The Relations between History and History of Science," 179–80, both in *Historical Studies Today*, ed. Gilbert and Graubard.
86. This is the criticism, developed with cogency and force, by Louis O. Mink, "Change and Causality in the History of Ideas," *Eighteenth Century Studies* 2, no. 1 (1969):7–25. See also the (not very illuminating) exchange that followed: Philip P. Wiener, "Some Remarks on Professor Mink's View of Methodology in the History of Ideas," ibid., 2, no. 3 (1969);311–17; Louis O. Mink, "Reply to Philip Wiener," ibid., 318–20.
87. Thus Mink, "Change and Causality," 13–16, and "Reply to Philip Wiener," 320; Thomas Bredsdorff, "Lovejoy's Idea of 'Ideas,'" *New Literary History* 8, no. 2 (1977);199–200. In his unhappy exchange with Lovejoy, Leo Spitzer, while not addressing this issue, lauded the *felix culpa* that led his colleague to produce in *Great Chain of Being*

21. Hamm, *Promissio, Pactum, Ordinatio,* 473–78, has shown that Alexander of Hales, who made use of the distinction around 1235 (see below, n. 31), was not the first to have done so.

22. Following in this the careful appraisal of William J. Courtenay, "Necessity and Freedom in Anselm's Concept of God," *Analecta anselmiana* 4, no. 2 (1975):39–64.

23. Albertus Magnus, *Summa theologiae,* pt. I, tract. XIX, qu. 78, membrum 2, in *Opera omnia,* ed. Auguste Borgnet, 36 vols. (Paris, 1890–99), 31:832–34. There is a good discussion of the meaning of the distinction for some of the earlier theologians as well as for William of Ockham in Jurgen Miethke, *Ockhams Weg zur Sozialphilosophie* (Berlin, 1969), 141–55. Cf. Mary Ann Pernoud, "Innovation in William of Ockham's References to the *Potentia Dei,*" *Antonianum* 45 (1970):65–97, and "The Theory of the *Potentia Dei* According to Aquinas, Scotus, and Ockham," ibid., 47 (1972);69–95.

24. Aquinas, *Summa theologiae,* Ia, qu. 25, art. 5. I cite here and below (though rarely without alteration) the translation of Thomas Gilby, *Summa theologiae,* 59 vols. (New York, 1964–76), 5:173.

25. These are the questions posed, respectively, in arts. 4, 5, and 6 of *Summa theologiae,* Ia, qu. 25.

26. *Summa theologiae,* Ia, qu. 25, art. 4 *sed contra,* art. 5 *resp.*

27. *Summa theologiae,* Ia, qu. 25, art. 5, trans. Gilby, 5:171.

28. See *Summa contra Gentiles,* III, 65, 69; cf. *Summa theologiae,* Ia, qu. 105, art. 5. The theologians in question are Al-Ash'arī (d. 935), his followers, and notably Al-Ghazālī (d. 1111). Aquinas was acquainted with versions of the views of these Mutakallimūn (dialecticians) via the accounts of them to be found in Moses Maimonides' *Guide to the Perplexed* and in the commentaries of Averroës on several of Aristotle's works; both were available to him in Latin translation. See Harry A. Wolfson, *The Philosophy of the Kalam* (Cambridge, Mass., 1976), 589–93. In the same work (518–600) Wolfson presents a carefully nuanced analysis of these views. See also Louis Gardet and M.-M. Anawati, *Introduction à la théologie musulmane* (Paris, 1948), 52–72 (a brief and general discussion), and Majid Fakhry, *Islamic Occasionalism and Its Critiques by Averroës and Aquinas* (London, 1958), esp. 56–82. Fakhry is perhaps too ready to assimilate these Muslim views to Malebranchian occasionalism; see the warning posted by William J. Courtenay, "The Critique on Natural Causality in the Mutakallimūn and Nominalism," *Harvard Theological Review* 66 (1973):77–94. On the point in question, Al-Ghazālī's arguments along with the replies of Averroes may be found in *Averroës' Tahafut al-Tahafut,* trans. Simon van den Bergh, 2 vols. (London, 1954), 1:316–33.

29. *Summa theologiae,* Ia, qu. 19, art. 4 (while at the same time Aquinas is careful to remind us that in God, will, understanding, and power are all one).

30. *Summa theologiae,* Ia, qu. 25, art. 5, trans. Gilby, 5:171.

31. *Alexandri de Hales . . . Summa theologica,* pars. I, inq. 1, tract. 4, qu. 1, c. 2, resp. 2, ed. P. P. Collegii S. Bonaventurae, 4 vols. (Quaracchi, 1924–48), 1:207, col. 2: "Distinguitur ergo potentia absoluta [a] potentia ordinata. Potentia absoluta est eorum quorum non est divina praeordinatione; potentia vero ordinata est eorum quorum est divina praeordinatio, hoc est eorum quae a Deo sunt praeordinata sive disposita."

32. Thus William J. Courtenay, "Nominalism and Late Medieval Religion," in *The Pursuit of Holiness in Late Medieval and Renaissance Religion,* ed. Charles Trinkaus and Heiko A. Oberman (Leiden, 1974), 39.

33. See esp. *Quodlibeta septem,* quodl. VI, qu. 1, ed. Joseph C. Wey, *Opera theologica* 9 of *Guillelmi de Ockham: Opera philosophica et theologica ad fidem codicem manuscriptorum edita* (St. Bonaventure, N.Y.: Franciscan Institute; 1980), 585–89; *Opus nonaginta dierum,* cap. 95, ed. R. F. Bennett and H. S. Offler, Vol. 2 of *Guillelmi de Ockham: Opera politica,* 3 vols. (Manchester, 1940–56), 715–29; *Tractatus contra Benedictum,* lib. III, cap. 3, ed. Offler, vol. 3 of *Guillelmi de Ockham: Opera politica,* 230–34. Cf. Courtenay, "Nominalism and Late Medieval Religion," 40–43; Gordon Leff, *William of Ockham: The Metamorphosis of Scholastic Discourse* (Manchester, 1975), 15–16, 450, 470–71; and, for somewhat different interpretations, Miethke, *Ockhams Weg zur Sozialphilosophie,* 146–56, and David W. Clark, "Ockham on Human and Divine Freedom," *Franciscan Studies* 38 (1978):122–60, who, without entirely disagreeing with him, frets (153n65) that "Courtenay has projected the confidence of St. Thomas about the permanence of God's ordained will and the present dispensation onto the doctrine of Ockham."

34. See his *De servo arbitrio* (1525), in *D. Martin Luthers Werke: Kritische Gesamtausgabe,* 91 vols. (Weimar, 1883–1980), 18:719.

35. William Ames, *The Marrow of Sacred Divinity,* bk. I, chap. 6, secs. 16–20, in *The Marrow of Theology,* ed. John D. Eusden (Boston, 1968), 93. For the publication history of the work, see Eusden's introduction, 1–3.

36. Samuel Willard, *A Compleat Body of Divinity* (Boston, 1726), qu. 4, serm. XXII, p. 70, col. 2.

37. See esp. *Tractatus contra Benedictum,* lib. III, cap. 3, ed. Offler, 234: "Et ideo, licet potentia Dei sit una, tamen propter diversam locutionem dicitur quod Deus aliqua potest de potentia absoluta, quae tam-

en numquam faciet de potentia ordinata (hoc est, de facto numquam faciet); *Opus nonaginta dierum*, cap. 95, in ibid., esp. 725–26.

38. Ockham, *Quodl.* VI, qu. 1, in *Quodlibeta septem*, ed. Wey, 585–86:

> . . . dico quod quaedam potest Deus facere de potentia ordinata, et aliqua de potentia absoluta. Haec distinctio non est sic intelligenda quod in Deo realiter sint duae potentiae quarum una sit ordinata et alia absoluta. Quia unica potentia est in Deo ad extra, quae omni modo est ipse Deus. Nec sic est intelligenda quod aliqua potest Deus ordinate facere, et aliqua potest absolute et non ordinate, quia Deus nihil potest facere inordinate.
>
> Sed est sic intelligenda quod "posse aliquid" quandoque accipitur secundum leges ordinatas et institutas a Deo, et illa dicitur Deus posse facere de potentia ordinata. Aliter accipitur "posse" pro posse facere omne illud quod non includit contradictionem fieri, sive Deus ordinaverit se hoc facturum sive non, quia multa potest Deus facere quae non vult facere . . . ; et illa dicitur Deus posse de potentia absoluta. Sicut Papa aliqua non potest secundum jura statuta ab eo, quae tamen absolute potest.
>
> Ista distinctio probatur per dictum Salvatoris, Joannis 3° 5: *Nisi quis* inquit *renatus fuerit ex aqua et Spiritu Sancto, non potest introire in regnum Dei.* Cum enim Deus sit aequalis potentiae nunc sicut prius, et aliquando aliqui introierunt in regnum Dei sine omni baptismo, sicut patet de pueris circumcisis tempore Legis defunctis antequam haberent usum rationis, et nunc est hoc possibile. Sed tamen illud quod tunc erat possibile secundum leges tunc institutas, nunc non est possibile secundum legem jam institutam, licet absolute sit possibile.

39. St. Peter Damiani, *Disputatio*, esp. cap. 10, in *Pierre Damien*, ed. Cantin, 428–32.

40. For this event (or rather process) and the problems with which it confronted philosophers, theologians, and ecclesiastical authorities alike, see Fernand van Steenberghen, *Aristotle in the West: The Origins of Latin Aristotelianism*, trans. Leonard Johnston (Louvain, 1955); John F. Wippel, "The Condemnations of 1270 and 1277 at Paris," *Journal of Medieval and Renaissance Studies* 7, no. 2 (1977):169–201.

41. Notably by Al-Ash'arī and Al-Ghazālī in the Muslim world (see above, n. 28).

42. Note, for example, the way Ockham handled the question that had brought Abelard to grief; see Armand Maurer, "Ockham on the Possibility of a Better World," *Mediaeval Studies* 38 (1976):291–312 (esp. 309–12). All, of course, were careful not to impugn the divine unicity and would agree with the commonplace sentiment expressed

later on by Pierre d'Ailly when he noted that "in God it is the same to will and to understand," just as all would agree with him that the distinction between the absolute and ordained powers does not denote the existence in God of two separate powers but is simply a human way of speaking about God's modes of action. See d'Ailly, *Quaestiones super I, III et IV Sententiarum* (Lyons, 1500), *Princ. in I Sent.*, R, fol. 26r, *Sent.* I, qu. 6, art. 2, L, fol. 97r, and *Sent.* I, qu. 13, art. 1, D, fol. 159r.

43. Aegidius Romanus, *De ecclesiastica potestate*, lib. III, caps. 2, 3, 7, and 9, ed. Richard Scholz (Weimar, 1929), 149–50, 152, 156–59, 181–82, 190–94.

44. John Duns Scotus, *Oxoniense scriptum in librum primum Sententiarum Magistri Petri Lombardi* (Coimbra, 1609), I, dist. 44, qu. *unica*, 677–78.

45. D'Ailly, *Sent.* I, qu. 13, art. 1 C–D, fols. 159r–159v.

46. *Sent.* I, qu. 9, art. 2 M, fol. 120r.

47. Ibid., qu. 1, art. 3 JJ, fol. 56r, and *Sent.* IV, qu. 1, art. 2 N, fol. 188r; *De Trinitate* and *De libertate creaturae rationalis*, in *Joannis Gersonii: Opera omnia*, ed. Louis Ellies Dupin, 5 vols. (Antwerp, 1706), 1:619, 632.

48. Francisco Suárez, *Metaphysicarum Disputationum*, disp. XXX, sec. 17, 2 vols. (Mainz, 1605), II, 140–41; also disp. XXXIV, sec. 7, II, 289, where he uses the phrase "de potentia absoluta, seu interveniente aliquo miraculo." Cf. his *De legibus ac Deo Legislatore*, lib. II, cap. 2, in *Selections from Three Works of Francis Suárez, S.J.*, 2 vols. (Oxford, 1944), 1:104, where he equates *secundum legem ordinariam* with *secundum potentiam ordinatam*.

49. Martin Luther, "*Vorlesungen über I Mose*," cap. 19, 14–20, and cap. 20, 2, in *Werke*, 43:71–82, 106 (esp. 71, where he says: "Sic ordinata potentia Dei est, quod aqua humectat, ignis urit etc. Sed in Babylone in medio igni Danielis socii incolumes vivebant. Haec fuit potentia Dei absoluta, secundum quam tum agebat, sed secundum hanc nihil nos jubet"). Luther delivered these lectures in 1535–36.

50. Thus, for example, Gabriel Biel (d. 1495) appears to equate God's operation *de potentia ordinata* with his operation *regulariter* and in accordance with "ordinatam et regularem suae voluntatis determinationem" (*Inventarium seu repertorium generale . . . super quattuor libros Sententiarum* [Lyons, 1519], IV, dist. 1, qu. 1 C; cf. ibid., L). Jacques Almain (d. 1516), *De penitentia . . . lectura*, fol. 6 v, col. 2, contrasts what can happen *de potentia absoluta* with what occurs "regulariter et de potentia ordinata"—included (with its own separate foliation) in *Aurea clarissimi et acutissimi Doctoris theologi Magistri Jacobi Almain Senonensis Opuscula* (Paris, 1918). John Major (d. 1550), *In*

primum Sententiarum (Paris, 1510), I, dist. 44, qu. unica, fol. ci v: The ordained power is "illa que est conformis legi ordinate que nobis constat per scripturam vel revelationem," comparable to a king's written law, which he (like God) can breach *de facto*. Sir Thomas More, *The Confutation of Tyndale's Answer*, 4, Y 3 v, contrasts God's "absolute power" with the "rule of his ordinary justyce"—in *The Complete Works of St. Thomas More*, ed. Richard S. Sylvester, 8 vols. (New Haven, 1963–), 7:569.

51. *In Primum Librum Sententiarum Annotatiunculae D. Johanne Eckio Praelectore*, ed. Walter L. Moore, Jr. (Leiden, 1976), dist. 42, pp. 122–26. Cf. dists. 43 and 44, pp. 127–28.

52. Ibid., dist. 42, p. 123.

53. Ames, *Marrow of Sacred Divinity*, I, chap. 6, p. 93 (Eusden renders *ordinata* as "ordaining").

54. Ibid., I, chap. 9, pp. 107–18. This usage is similar to that adopted by Dudley Fenner in what may have been the first of the methodical *summae* of theology to circulate among the English Puritans—*Sacra Theologia sive Veritas* (Geneva, 1589), II, cap. 10, fol. 18r. Cf. William Perkins, *A Resolution to the Countrey-man*, in *The Workes of That Famous and Worthy Minister of Christ . . . M. W. Perkins*, 3 vols. (Cambridge, 1608–31), 3:657, where he contrasts the "general providence" whereby God works by means of secondary causes and that immediate governance of the world whereby "his providence worketh without means, and many things . . . bringeth to passe against all meanes."

55. Increase Mather, *The Doctrine of Divine Providence Opened and Applyed* (Boston, 1684), 45–47; Thomas Shepard, *Three Valuable Pieces viz. Select Cases Resolved: Of the Oracles of God, or, Sum of Christian Religion . . . and A Private Diary* (Boston, 1747), 9–10 (the work was written in 1647).

56. John Norton, *The Orthodox Evangelis or a Treatise wherein many Great Evangelical Truths are briefly Discussed, cleared and confirmed* (London, 1654), 19–20 (for God's "absolute and unlimited" vs. "ordinate and limited" powers) and 103–4 (for God's "ordinary" and "extraordinary" governance of the world); Samuel Willard, *A Compleat Body of Divinity*, qu. 4, sermon XXII, p. 70 (for "unlimited and absolute power" vs. "ordinate power"), and qu. 11, sermon XLIV, pp. 136–38 (for "ordinary" vs. "extraordinary" providence).

57. Thus Perkins, *An Exposition of the Symbole of the Creed of the Apostles*, in *Workes*, 1:159; *A Resolution to the Countrey-man*, in *Workes*, 3:657; *A Discourse of the Damned Art of Witchcraft*, in *Workes*, 3:609; Increase Mather, *Doctrine of Divine Providence*, 24,

53–54, 64; Shepard, *Three Valuable Pieces*, 10; Preston, *Life Eternall*, 200; Norton, *Orthodox Evangelis*, 124; Willard, *Compleat Body of Divinity*, qu. 11, serm. XLVI, p. 144.

58. Ockham, *Opus nonaginta dierum*, cap. 95, in *Opera politica*, ed. Bennett and Offler, 2:278; *Tractatus contra Benedictum*, lib. III, cap. 3, in ibid., 3:234.

59. On this matter, see especially the helpful discussion in Courtenay, "Nominalism and Late Medieval Religion," 37–43, and in Miethke, *Ockhams Weg zur Sozialphilosophie*, 141–56.

60. See Maurice de Wulf, *Histoire de la philosophie médiévale*, 3 vols., 6th ed. (Paris, 1947), 3:47; Gordon Leff, *Bradwardine and the Pelagians* (Cambridge, Eng., 1957), 132, and *Medieval Thought from St. Augustine to Ockham* (Harmondsworth, 1958), 289; Erwin Iserloh, *Gnade und Eucharistie in der philosophischen Theologie des Wilhelm von Ockham* (Wiesbaden, 1956), 67–79; Werner Dettloff, *Die Entwicklung der Akzeptations- und Verdienstlehre von Duns Scotus bis Luther* (Münster, 1963), 363–65. Leff has since distanced himself from Iserloh's interpretation and has indicated his wish to distinguish the use made of the distinction by Ockham himself from the more radical use to which his "followers and successors" put it; see his *William of Ockham*, esp. 15–16, 450, 470–71.

61. For the distinction and the claims of the mystics, see Steven E. Ozment, "Mysticism, Nominalism, and Dissent," in *Pursuit of Holiness*, ed. Trinkaus and Oberman, 67–92 (esp. 80–92), and *Mysticism and Dissent: Religious Ideology and Social Protest in the Sixteenth Century* (New Haven, 1973), esp. 1–60. For the use of the distinction by the lawyers, see below, chap. 4. It has recently been claimed that the distinction also generated some echoes in one of the fourteenth-century English mystery cycles; see Kathleen M. Ashley, "Divine Power in Chester Cycle and Late Medieval Thought," *Journal of the History of Ideas* 39, no. 3 (1978):387–404, as also the subsequent exchange in vol. 40, no. 3 (1979), of the same journal: James R. Royse, "Nominalism and Divine Power in the Chester Cycle," 475–76, and Kathleen Ashley, "Chester Cycle and Nominalist Thought," 477.

62. D'Ailly, "Sermo de sancto dominico" and "Sermo de quadruplici adventu domini," in *Tractatus et sermones* (Strassburg, 1491), sig. C4v and t5v–t6r; John W. O'Malley, "Preaching for the Popes," in *Pursuit of Holiness*, ed. Trinkaus and Oberman, 415; cf. E. Jane Dempsey Douglass, *Justification in Late Medieval Preaching: A Study of John Geiler of Keisersberg* (Leiden, 1966), 82, 163–65. Geiler apparently made use of the idea but not the technical terminology. For the use of the distinction by More, Fenner, Ames, Willard, and other Puritans, see above, nn. 50, 53, 54, 55, 56.

63. Ockham, *Tractatus contra Benedictum*, lib. III, cap. 3, in *Opera politica*, ed. Bennett and Offler, 3:230.

64. See esp. Heiko Oberman, "Wir sein pettler. Hoc est verum. Bund und Gnade in der Theologie des Mittelalters und der Reformation," *Zeitschrift für Kirchengeschichte* 78 (1967):232–52; Martin Greschat, "Der Bundesgedanke in der Theologie des späten Mittelalters," ibid., 81 (1970):44–63; William J. Courtenay, "Covenant and Causality in Pierre d'Ailly," *Speculum* 46, no. 1 (1971):94–119; Hamm, *Promissio, Pactum, Ordinatio*, esp. 473–95. Clark, "Ockham on Human and Divine Freedom," 149–60, mounts (in relation solely to Ockham) an "implicit" but rather wavering criticism of the "covenantal" interpretation of the two powers.

65. See the brief account in Heiko A. Oberman, ed., *Forerunners of the Reformation: The Shape of Late Medieval Thought* (New York, 1966), 130–40, and the more detailed analysis in his *The Harvest of Medieval Theology: Gabriel Biel and Late Medieval Nominalism* (Cambridge, Mass., 1963), 185–248.

66. Citing here Courtenay, "Covenant and Causality in Pierre d'Ailly," 98, and prescinding from the disagreements among scholars concerning the extent to which Aquinas ascribed *physical* causality to the sacraments. For the extensive literature on that subject, see Courtenay, 98n13.

67. See *Summa theologiae*, IIa IIae, qu. 23, art. 2; Ia IIae, qu. 110, art. 2.

68. Steven Ozment, *The Age of Reform, 1250–1550: An Intellectual and Religious History of Late Medieval and Reformation Europe* (New Haven, 1980), 33. My remarks here and in what follows are dependent on Ozment and on Courtenay, "Covenant and Causality in Pierre d'Ailly," both of them splendidly lucid accounts, and, more generally, on Paul Vignaux, *Justification et Prédestination au XIVe siècle* (Paris, 1934).

69. Courtenay, "Covenant and Causality in Pierre d'Ailly," 99. For the development and significance of the analogy of the king and the leaden coin, see his "The King and the Leaden Coin: The Economic Background of 'Sine qua Non' Causality," *Traditio* 28 (1972):185–209.

70. Ozment, *Age of Reform*, 244.

71. Robert Holcot, *Super libros Sapientiae* (Hagenau, 1494), lect. 145B; I cite the translation by Paul Nyhus in *Forerunners of the Reformation: The Shape of Late Medieval Thought*, ed. Heiko Oberman (New York, 1966), 149.

72. Ockham, *Quodl*. VI, qu. 6, in *Quodlibeta septem*, ed. Wey, 605; cf. D'Ailly, *Princ. in I Sent.*, K, fol. 23v.

73. Ockham, *Quodl*. VI, qu. 6, in *Quodlibeta septem*, ed. Wey,

604–6; *Reportatio* II, qu. 15 E, in "The Notitia Intuitiva of Non-Exis-
tents According to William Ockham," ed. Philotheus Boehner, *Traditio*
1 (1943):248–50. Cf. D'Ailly, *Sent.*, I, qu. 3, art. 1, M, fol. 72v, for the
same claim. There are good recent discussions of the issue in Marilyn
M. Adams, "Intuitive Cognition, Certainty, and Scepticism in William
of Ockham," *Traditio* 26 (1970):389–98, and John F. Boler, "Intuitive
and Abstractive Cognition," in *The Cambridge History of Later Medieval Philosophy*, ed. Kretzmann et al., 460–78.

3. Nebuchadnezzar's Fiery Furnace

1. William Irvine, *Apes, Angels, and Victorians* (New York, 1955),
6.
2. See esp. W. E. H. Lecky, *History of the Rise and Influence of the
Spirit of Rationalism in Europe*, 2 vols. (London, 1865), by no means
hostile to religion but highly critical of the theological dogmatism that
was the heritage of the seventeenth century from the Middle Ages and
Reformation era alike.
3. John W. Draper, *History of the Conflict between Religion and
Science* (New York, 1875).
4. Andrew D. White, *The Warfare of Science* (New York, 1876), 7.
White eventually expanded the book into *A History of the Warfare of
Science with Theology in Christendom*, 2 vols. (New York, 1896).
5. As, in some measure, E. A. Burtt's fine book, *The Metaphysical
Foundations of Modern Physical Science* (London, 1925). Also Richard
F. Jones, *Ancients and Moderns* (St. Louis, 1936): Basil Willey, *The
Seventeenth Century Background* (London, 1934), on which see the
comments of Richard S. Westfall, *Science and Religion in Seventeenth-
Century England* (New Haven, 1958), 223–24.
6. Notably Westfall, *Science and Religion*, and R. Hooykaas, *Religion and the Rise of Modern Science* (Edinburgh, 1972).
7. Robert Boyle, *The Christian Virtuoso*, in *The Works of the Hon-
ourable Robert Boyle*, ed. Thomas Birch, new ed., 6 vols. (London,
1972), 5:513, speaks of the *virtuosi* as "those that understand and culti-
vate experimental philosophy."
8. Westfall, *Science and Religion*, 23–24 (citing Henry Stubbe, *The
Plus Ultra Reduced to a Nonplus* [London, 1670], 172–73).
9. See Harcourt Brown, *Scientific Organizations in Seventeenth
Century France* (Baltimore, 1934), 255–57; Westfall, *Science and Religion*, 23 and n. 17.
10. Franklin L. Baumer, *Religion and the Rise of Scepticism* (New
York, 1960), 79–95. Similarly Burtt, *Metaphysical Foundations*; Westfall, *Science and Religion*; and others.

11. See the pertinent comments of J. E. McGuire, "Boyle's Conception of Nature," *Journal of the History of Ideas* 33, no. 4 (1972):524.

12. Marie Boas, *Robert Boyle and Seventeenth-Century Chemistry* (Cambridge, Eng., 1958), 229–32.

13. McGuire, "Boyle's Conception of Nature," 526. Cf. the comparable sentiments expressed in Boas, *Robert Boyle*, 229; Burtt, *Metaphysical Foundations*, 160; Westfall, *Science and Religion*, 17, 73.

14. Thomas Birch, "The Life of the Author," which he prefixes to *Works*, 1:cxxxviii.

15. In the title to one of his works: *Some Considerations about the Reconcileableness of Reason and Religion*, in *Works*, ed. Birch, 4:151–91.

16. In *Works*, ed. Birch, 5:508–40.

17. Mitchell S. Fisher, *Robert Boyle: Devout Naturalist* (Philadelphia, 1945); Richard M. Hunt, *The Place of Religion in the Science of Robert Boyle* (Pittsburgh, 1955).

18. Notably Westfall, *Science and Religion*, esp. 83–92; Baumer, *Religion and the Rise of Scepticism*, 78–90. Cf. Burtt, *Metaphysical Foundations*, 187–96, and Barbara J. Shapiro, *Probability and Certainty in Seventeenth-Century England* (Princeton, 1983), 93, for somewhat less explicitly skeptical appraisals.

19. Baumer, *Religion and the Rise of Scepticism*, 84; Burtt, *Metaphysical Foundations*, 196.

20. Westfall, *Science and Religion*, 89.

21. See esp. Leibniz's first and second paper and Clarke's first and second reply, in *The Leibniz-Clarke Correspondence*, ed. H. G. Alexander (Manchester, 1956), 11–14, 17–20, 22–24. Cf. Alexander's comment on the issue, "Introduction," xvi–xviii, and J. E. McGuire, "Force, Active Principles, and Newton's Invisible Realm," *Ambix* 15, no. 3 (1968):154–208 (stressing the fluctuations across time in Newton's understanding of "active principles").

22. Baumer, *Religion and the Rise of Scepticism*, 85.

23. *A Free Inquiry into the Vulgarly Received Notion of Nature*, in *Works*, ed. Birch, 5:197; *On the Excellency and Grounds of the Corpuscular or Mechanical Philosophy*, in ibid., 4:68.

24. *Christian Virtuoso*, in *Works*, ed. Birch, 5:521.

25. *Free Inquiry*, in *Works*, ed. Birch, 5:216, 223.

26. *Some Considerations*, in *Works*, ed. Birch, 4:159, 161.

27. *Of the High Veneration Man's Intellect Owes to God*, in *Works*, ed. Birch, 5:149.

28. *Free Inquiry*, in *Works*, ed. Birch, 5:170.

29. Ibid., 163–64.

30. *Some Considerations*, in *Works*, ed. Birch, 4:161–62. He also cites on two other occasions, as an illustration of God's exercise of his

absolute power, the miraculous delivery of the three youths from the fiery furnace; see *Some Physico-theological Considerations about the Possibility of the Resurrection*, in ibid., 4:201–2, and *A Disquisition about the Final Causes of Natural Things*, in ibid., 5:412.

31. I.e., possessed of no intrinsic causal efficacy but functioning under customary circumstances as conditions *sine qua non*. See above, chap. 2 pp. 63–64. Cf. Harry A. Wolfson, *The Philosophy of the Kalam* (Cambridge, Mass., 1976), 544–51. I remain unpersuaded by the suggestion of William J. Courtenay, "The Critique of Natural Causality in the Mutakallimūn and Nominalism," *Harvard Theological Review* 66 (1973);85–86, that al-Ghazālī, at least, also toyed with an alternative theory of causality *ex natura rei*.

32. A. N. Whitehead, *Science and the Modern World* (New York, 1958), chap. 1.

33. Nicholas' writings survive in fragmentary form and it is not always easy to identify the particular position to which he adheres. See J. Reginald O'Donnell, "The Philosophy of Nicholas of Autrecourt and His Appraisal of Aristotle," *Mediaeval Studies* 4 (1942):97–125; Julius R. Weinberg, *Nicolaus of Autrecourt: A Study in 14th Century Thought* (Princeton, 1948).

34. See Ernest A. Moody, "Ockham, Buridan, and Nicholas of Autrecourt," *Franciscan Studies* 7 (1947):113–46; T. K. Scott, Jr., "Nicholas of Autrecourt, Buridan, and Ockhamism," *Journal of the History of Philosophy* 9 (1971):15–41. This issue of doctrinal affiliations is an exceedingly complex one and it has not yielded readily to resolution. Thus Scott, for example, can argue that while Nicholas' critique of causal knowledge does indeed set him at odds with Ockham as well as with Buridan (37), his "understanding of the nature and criteria of knowing is nearer Ockham's than is Buridan's" (15).

35. *In metaphysicen Aristotelis Quaestiones argutissimae Magistri Joannis Buridani* (Paris, 1518), II, qu. 1, fol. 9r; cited in Moody, "Ockham, Buridan, and Nicholas of Autrecourt," 140n40.

36. Moody, "Ockham, Buridan, and Nicholas of Autrecourt," 135.

37. Just as, in Ockham's case, it had involved a comparably significant shift in his understanding of the functioning of sacramental grace in the economy of salvation. See above, chap. 2, pp. 63–64.

38. R. G. Collingwood, *The Idea of Nature* (Oxford, 1945), 3–9.

39. *Summa theologiae* Ia IIae, qu. 91, arts. 1 and 2; qu. 93, art. 1. Cf. Francis Oakley, "Medieval Theories of Natural Law: William of Ockham and the Significance of the Voluntarist Tradition," *Natural Law Forum* 6 (1961):67–68.

40. Thus Pierre d'Ailly, while conceding that the divine will and intellect can be distinguished neither really nor formally, argues that

such a distinction can be regarded as the abbreviated expression of something true. And in accordance with "the way of speaking of the saints and doctors," it is more correct to regard the divine will than the divine intellect as the first obligatory law in the order of morality, since the divine will is the effective cause of things whereas the divine intellect is not, in that whatever that will decrees actually comes to pass, but not whatever that intellect comprehends. See Francis Oakley, *The Political Thought of Pierre d'Ailly* (New Haven, 1964), 182–84, where the pertinent texts are cited.

41. For Ockham, see Oakley, "Medieval Theories of Natural Law," 68–72, and for d'Ailly, Oakley, *Political Thought of Pierre d'Ailly*, 182–96. For arguments in favor of qualifying in varying degree the ascription of a "voluntarist" position to Ockham, see David W. Clarke, "Voluntarism and Rationalism in the Ethics of Ockham," *Franciscan Studies* 31 (1971):72–87; Linwood Urban, "William of Ockham's Theological Ethics," *Franciscan Studies* 33 (1973):310–50. Neither of these interesting articles pays sufficient attention, I judge, to the role played in Ockham's arguments by his assumption of the distinction between the *potentia dei absoluta et ordinata*.

42. *Guillelmi de Ockham: Quaestiones in Librum Secundum Sententiarum (Reportatio)*, qu. III–IV and XV, ed. Gedeon Gál and Rega Wood, *Opera theologica* 5 of *Guillelmi de Ockham: Opera philosophica et theologica ad fidem codicem manuscriptorum edita* (St. Bonaventure, N.Y.: Franciscan Institute 1981), 59, 352.

43. Ibid., qu. XV, 353.

44. A fact underlined by Ockham's use of such qualifications as *stante ordinatione quae nunc est* and *stante ordinatione divina;* see Ockham, *Super quatuor libros Sententiarum* (Lyons: Jean Trechsel, 1495), III, 12 CCC. Cf. Pierre d'Ailly, *Quaestiones super I, III et IV Sententiarum* (Lyons: Nicolaus Wolff, 1500), *Princ. in I Sent.*, H, fol. 22v; K, fol. 23v.

45. See esp. *Guillelmi de Ockham: Scriptum in Librum Primum Sententiarum Ordinatio*, dist. 41, qu. unica, ed. Giraldus I. Etzkorn and Franciscus E. Kelley, *Opera theologica* 4 (1979):609–10; *Sent. III*, 13C (Lyons ed.). Cf. d'Ailly, *Princ. in II Sent.*, P, fol. 31r–31v. In this connection Heiko A. Oberman's remarks about the cognate views of Gabriel Biel (d. 1495) are apposite: "In the thesis that God is the first rule of all justice, it is not the lawlessness of the set order which is expressed, but man's inability to discover the motives and causes of God's actions" (*The Harvest of Medieval Theology: Gabriel Biel and Late Medieval Nominalism* [Cambridge, Mass., 1963], 98).

46. See Oakley, "Medieval Theories of Natural Law," 72–73, and "Christian Theology and the Newtonian Science: The Rise of the Con-

07

cept of the Laws of Nature," *Church History* 30, no. 4 (1961):433–57. For the argument on Locke's position, see Francis Oakley and Elliott W. Urdang, "Locke, Natural Law, and God," *Natural Law Forum* 11 (1966):92–109.

47. See above, chap. 2, p. 52.

48. D'Ailly, *Sent.* I, qu. 14, art. 3, Q, fol. 173r; *Princ. in I Sent.*, D, fol. 21r, and J, fol. 23r; *Princ. in II Sent.*, J, fol. 29r; *Princ. in IV Sent.*, L, fol. 41v.

49. D'Ailly, *De libertate creaturae rationalis* and *De Trinitate*, in Jean Gerson, *Opera omnia*, ed. Louis Ellies Dupin, 5 vols. (Antwerp, 1706), 1:632, 619; *Sent.* I, qu. 1, art. 2, JJ, fol. 96r. D'Ailly also uses the expressions "by the natural or naturally ordained power" in contrast with "supernaturally . . . or by the absolute power" (*Sent.* IV, qu. 1, art. 2, J, fol. 188r).

50. *Sent.* IV, qu. 1, art. 1, N, fol. 188r; *Tractatus de legibus et sectis*, in Gerson, *Opera omnia*, ed. Dupin, 1:793.

51. This would certainly appear to have been the case with Buridan, whom Anneliese Maier has described as putting in place of final causes in the investigation of natural phenomena "nothing other than natural law in the modern sense" (*Metaphysische Hintergründe der Spätscholastischen Naturphilosophie* [Rome, 1955], 381).

52. See John E. Murdoch, "From Social into Intellectual Factors: An Aspect of the Unitary Character of Late Medieval Learning," in *The Cultural Context of Medieval Learning*, ed. J. E. Murdoch and E. D. Sylla (Boston, 1975), 271–348 (esp. 281, 292, 297–300, 312, 314n23, 326–27n 101, 333–34nn122 and 126; Murdoch, "Infinity and Continuity," in *The Cambridge History of Later Medieval Philosophy*, ed. Norman Kretzmann, Anthony Kenny, and Jan Pinborg (Cambridge, Eng., 1982), 566–69; Anneliese Maier, *Die Vorläufer Galileis im 14. Jahrhundert: Studien zur Naturphilosophie der Spätscholastik* (Rome, 1949), esp. 155–215; Maier, *Metaphysische Hintergründe*, 381; Edward Grant, "The Condemnation of 1277, God's Absolute Power, and Physical Thought in the Late Middle Ages," *Viator* 10 (1979):211–44.

53. See above, n. 35.

54. See William J. Courtenay, "Covenant and Causality in Pierre d'Ailly," *Speculum* 46, no. 1 (1971):116–19.

55. Eugene M. Klaaren, *Religious Origins of Modern Science* (Grand Rapids, Mich., 1977), 137.

56. James I, "A Speach to the Lords and Commons of the Parliament at White-Hall," March 21, 1609, in *The Political Works of James I*, ed. Charles H. McIlwain (Cambridge, Mass., 1918), 309.

57. William Ames, *The Marrow of Sacred Divinity*, bk. I, chap. 9, §10, in *The Marrow of Theology*, ed. John D. Eusden (Boston, 1968), 108.

58. Francis Bacon, *A Confession of Faith*, in *The Works of Francis Bacon*, ed. James Spedding et al., 14 vols. (London, 1857–74), 7:219–26; René Descartes, *Meditationes de prima philosophia*, in *Oeuvres des Descartes*, ed. Charles Adam and Paul Tannery, 13 vols. (Paris, 1897–1910), 7:434–35. For Newton (who, unlike Descartes, does not use the precise terminology), see McGuire, "Force, Active Principles, and Newton's Invisible Realm," 190–91, where he cites a pertinent passage from one of the Newton manuscripts.

59. See Oakley, "Christian Theology and the Newtonian Science."

60. The less so in that it has drawn added support from the researches of McGuire, "Force, Active Principles, and Newton's Invisible Realm" and "Boyle's Conception of Nature"; Klaaren, *Religious Origins of Modern Science*; and Margaret J. Osler, "Descartes and Charleton on Nature and God," *Journal of the History of Ideas* 40, no. 3 (1979):445–56. Cf. Edward Grant, *Physical Science in the Middle Ages* (New York, 1971); Hooykaas, *Religion and the Rise of Modern Science*, esp. 7–28; and Michael Heyd, "From a Rationalist Theology of Cartesian Voluntarism: David Derodon and Jean-Robert Chouet," *Journal of the History of Ideas* 40, no. 4 (1979): 527–42. My only real reservation concerns my failure to come up with a better term to designate the tradition in question than "voluntarist"—a label that appears to suggest misleadingly that one is incorrectly emphasizing the arbitrariness or intrinsic "irrationality" of God's activity *ad extra* rather than its freedom, its inscrutability, and its transcendence of the categories of any merely human rationality.

61. Ralph Cudworth, *Treatise Concerning Immutable Morality* (New York, 1838), bk. I, chaps. 1 and 3, pp. 9–11, 18.

62. Thus (and the texts deserve citing) Descartes, Letter to Mersenne, April 15, 1630, in *Oeuvres de Descartes*, ed. Adam and Tannery, 1:145:

> Mais je ne laisseray pas de toucher en ma Physique plusieurs questions metaphysiques, et particulieremant celle-cy: Que les verités mathematiques, lesquelles vous nommés eternelles, ont esté establies de Dieu et en dependent entieremant, aussy bien que tout le reste des creatures. C'est en effait parler de Dieu comme d'un Juppiter ou Saturne, et l'assuiettir au Stix et aus destinees, que de dire que ces verités sont independantes de luy. Ne craignés point, je vous prie, d'assurer et de publier par tout, que c'est Dieu qui a establi ces lois en la nature, ainsy qu'un Roy establist des lois en son Royausme.

Also Descartes [to Mersenne?], May 27, 1630, in ibid., 151–52:

> Vous me demandez *in quo genere causae Deus disposuit aeternas veritates*. Je vous répons que c'est *in eodem genere causae* qu'il a

crée toutes choses, c'est à dire *ut efficiens et totalis causa.* Car il est
certain qu'il est aussi bien Autheur de l'essence comme de l'existence des creatures: ou cette essence n'est autre chose que ces veritez eternelles, lesquelles je ne conçoy point émaner de Dieu, comme les rayons de Soleil. . . . Vous demandez aussi qui a necessité
Dieu à creer ces veritez; et je dis qu'il a esté aussi libre de faire qu'il
ne fust pas vray que toutes les lignes tirées du centre à la circon-
ference fussent égales, comme de ne pas creer le monde.

Meditationes de prima philosophia, in ibid., VII, 436:

Nec opus etiam est quaerere qua ratione Deus potuisset ab aeterno
facere, ut non fuisset verum, bis 4 esse 8, etc.; fateor enim id a nobis
intelligi non posse. . . . Nec proinde putandum est *aeternas veri-
tates pendere ab humano intellectu, vel ab aliis rebus existentibus,*
sed a solo Deo, qui ipsas ab aeterno, ut summus legislator, instituit.

Harry Frankfurt, "Descartes on the Creation of the Eternal Truths,"
Philosophical Review 86, no. 1 (1977):36–57, argues convincingly (and
pace Koyré) that such sentiments are not to be dismissed as "a tempo-
rary aberration" in Descartes's thinking but reflect his controlling
convictions.

63. Boyle, *A Disquisition about the Final Causes of Natural
Things,* in *Works,* ed. Birch, 5:401.

64. McGuire, "Boyle's Conception of Nature," 538; cf. Robert Kar-
gon, "Walter Charleton, Robert Boyle, and the Acceptance of Epicurean
Atomism in England," *Isis* 55 (1964):184–92.

65. Walter Charleton, *The Darknes of Atheism Dispelled by the
Light of Nature: A Physico-theologicall Treatise* (London, 1652),
125, 152, 329.

66. Locke, *Essays on the Law of Nature,* ed. W. van Leyden (Oxford,
1954), Essay I, 108–10.

67. Sir Isaac Newton, *Philosophiae Naturalis Principia Mathematica: Scholium Generale,* in *Opera quae exstant omnia,* ed. Samuel
Horsley, 5 vols. (London, 1779–85), 3:170–74; *Optics,* in ibid., 4:263.
Also Newton's earlier draft of the ideas he later expressed in the General Scholium (cited by McGuire, "Force, Active Principles, and Newton's Invisible Realm," 190), and by A. R. and M. B. Hall, *Unpublished
Scientific Papers of Isaac Newton* (Cambridge, Eng., 1962), 138–39).

68. I note with interest the similar conclusion arrived at (via a
rather different route) by R. M. Burns, *The Great Debate on Miracles
from Joseph Glanvill to David Hume* (London, 1981), 51–57 and
247–51, where he criticizes Westfall's interpretation on this point of
Nehemiah Grew, Edmond Halley, and Thomas Sydenham, and argues

(52) that Westfall, "convinced (because of the influence of ideas which became current only at a later period) of the inevitability of conflict between the scientific attitude and miracles, has read into Boyle's writings 'contradictions' and 'conflicts' for which there is no substantial evidence."

69. Boyle, *The Christian Virtuoso,* in *Works,* ed. Birch, 5:521; *A Free Inquiry,* in ibid., 170–71.

70. Francisco Suárez, *De Legibus ac Deo Legislatore,* lib. I, cap. 1, and lib. II, cap. 2, in *Selections from Three Works of Francisco Suárez, S. J.,* 2 vols. (Oxford, 1944), 1:8 and 104; *Metaphysicarum Disputationum,* 2 vols., disp. XXII, sect. 4, XXX, sect. 17 (Mainz, 1605), 1:568–69 and 2:150.

71. The terms he uses are *potentia dei ordinaria et extraordinaria.* See *Meditationes de prima philosophia,* Resp. ad sextas objectiones, in *Oeuvres de Descartes,* ed. Adam and Tannery, 7:435.

72. See McGuire, "Boyle's Conception of Nature," 530; cf. his "Force, Active Principles, and Newton's Invisible Realm," 201.

73. McGuire, "Force, Active Principles, and Newton's Invisible Realm," 206–7, citing Newton's *Opticks.*

74. Lovejoy, *Great Chain of Being,* 144–82; cf. 307n7.

75. Which blasphemously coerces "his infinite and arbitrary Activity with the definite laws of second causes" and denies "him the prerogative of absolute superiority to his mechanîque Vicegerent, or (rather) Instrument, Nature" (Charleton, *Darknes of Atheism,* 217).

76. See above, n. 62.

77. *Principia mathematica,* in *Opera omnia,* ed. Horsley, 2:xx, xxiii.

78. Boyle, *Free Inquiry,* in *Works,* ed. Birch, 5:195–96, 163–64. Earlier in the century, interestingly, in defending Galileo against his Aristotelian detractors, Thomas Campanella noted that Aquinas' attempt to synthesize Aristotelian philosophy and Christian theology had been "rebuked in the Articles of Paris" (Grant, "Condemnation of 1277," 242n131).

79. The importance of bringing to an understanding of these worries some sense of the larger philosophical and theological context I have been trying to describe is well (if unfortunately) underlined by the redundant puzzlement of J. R. Jacob, *Robert Boyle and the English Revolution: A Study in Social and Intellectual Change* (New York, 1977), 161, about Boyle's purpose in writing *A Free Inquiry into the Vulgarly Received Notion of Nature.* "Why," Jacob asks, "was Boyle so concerned to oppose his natural philosophy to the vulgarly received notion [of nature]? Was Aristotelian and Platonic philosophy in 1666 tainted with heresy and atheism? If so, how could this be? For centuries

Aristotle had been at the foundations of orthodox Christian thought."
And the drawbacks of too exclusive a concern with "ideological origins" are equally well underlined by Jacob's willingness, in the absence
of any supporting textual evidence (and in the teeth of Boyle's own
constant identification of Aristotelian ideas as his primary target), to
insist (161–76) that his quarrel in *A Free Inquiry* was "less with Aristotle and his scholastic interpreters than with certain contemporaries,"
notably the group associated with John Heydon, who moved in court
circles in the 1660s, was connected with the second duke of Buck-
ingham, and was accused of plotting sedition. One must be forgiven for
harboring some doubts about the "gain in historicity" which Jacob
(4–5) is bold enough to claim for his approach.

80. See William B. Hunter, Jr., "The Seventeenth Century Doctrine
of Plastic Nature," *Harvard Theological Review* 42, no. 3 (1950):
197–213; Westfall, *Science and Religion*, 84–89. Cf. Alexandre Koyré,
From the Closed World to the Infinite Universe (Baltimore, 1957),
125–54. For recent work on More and the Cambridge Platonists, see C.
A. Staudenbauer, "Platonism, Theosophy, and Immaterialism: Recent
Views of the Cambridge Platonists," *Journal of the History of Ideas* 35,
no. 1 (1974):157–69.

81. Boyle, *Free Inquiry*, in *Works*, ed. Birch, 5:esp. 164, 167, 173,
221, 241, 250.

82. Ibid., 158–254; the phrase in question occurs at 216.

83. Leibniz, *De ipsa natura*, §2, in *Die philosophischen Schriften
von Gottfried Wilhelm Leibniz*, ed. C. J. Gerhardt, 7 vols. (Berlin,
1875–90), 4:505.

84. Ibid., §§3 and 5, 4:505–7.

85. Ibid., §§2, 5, 7 and 9, 4:505, 507–9.

86. Ibid., §§11 and 13, 4:511, 514.

87. See McGuire, "Boyle's Conception of Nature," 539. Though the
focus of her concern is different from mine, Carolyn Merchant, *The
Death of Nature: Women, Ecology, and the Scientific Revolution* (New
York, 1980), 275–89, arrives at a similar appraisal of Leibniz' position.

88. Not least in the thinking of Newton himself, which, voluntarist
though it was, bore also the imprint of More's view of nature. See
Koyré, *From the Closed World*, 190; J. E. McGuire, "Neoplatonism and
Active Principles: Newton and the Corpus Hermeticum," in *Hermeti-
cism and the Scientific Revolution*, ed. Robert W. Westman and J. E.
McGuire (Los Angeles, 1977), 93–142, esp. 93–105. Similarly Leibniz,
whose sympathies extended not only to some of More's views but even
to the "monistic vitalism" of More's friend the younger Helmont; see
Carolyn Merchant, "The Vitalism of Francis Mercury Van Helmont:
His Influence on Leibniz," *Ambix* 26, no. 3 (1979):170–83.

89. See Leibniz' first and second papers and Clarke's first reply, in *Leibniz-Clarke Correspondence,* ed. Alexander, 11–12, 14, 19–20. Cf. Koyré, *From the Closed World,* 235–76.

90. Since I posed this question I have come across two articles that focus intriguingly on the parallelisms in question and affirm their *political* significance; see Steven Shapin, "Of Gods and Kings: Natural Philosophy and Politics in the Leibniz-Clarke Disputes," *Isis* 72 (June 1981):187–215, and (a briefer statement) Shapin, "Licking Leibniz," *History of Science* 19 (1981):298–99. Shapin sees such parallelisms as witnessing to the degree to which "late seventeenth- and early eighteenth-century conceptions of God's attributes and his role in nature functioned in overtly political as well as natural-philosophical and theological settings," "conflicting conceptions of political and moral order" being "sustained by the invocation of diverging notions of divine and natural order." Happily, the argument I pursue in the next chapter harmonizes very well with Shapin's claims. It does make clear, however, that the argumentative tactic he describes was not limited to the period with which he is concerned, but had enjoyed a long prehistory stretching back via the early seventeenth century well into the Middle Ages.

4. Divine Sovereignty, Papal Miracle, Royal Grace

1. J. N. Figgis, *Studies of Political Thought from Gerson to Grotius,* 2d ed. (Cambridge, Eng., 1931), 60.

2. See Peter Laslett's introduction to his critical edition of *John Locke: Two Treatises of Government* (Cambridge, Eng., 1968), esp. 67–78.

3. J. N. Figgis, *The Divine Right of Kings,* Torchbook ed. (New York, 1965), 1; italics mine. (The book was first published in 1896.)

4. Charles Howard McIlwain, ed., *The Political Works of James I* (Cambridge, Mass., 1918).

5. This is the judgment of David Harris Willson, *King James VI and I* (New York, 1956), 168.

6. Their "often racy, pungent, and picturesque prose" notwithstanding (see Willson, *King James VI and I,* 68.

7. Thus J. W. Allen, *A History of Political Thought in the Sixteenth Century,* 2d ed. (London, 1941), 253; George H. Sabine, *A History of Political Theory,* rev. ed. (London, 1959), 393–94; most particularly McIlwain, ed., *Political Works of James I,* xxxvii–xliii. Cf. the dissenting comment of W. H. Greenleaf, "James I and the Divine Right of Kings," *Political Studies* 5 (1957):37, 44n2.

8. Greenleaf, "James I and the Divine Right of Kings," 48. Also his *Order, Empiricism, and Politics: Two Traditions of English Political Thought, 1500–1700* (London, 1964), esp. 67; his "The Thomasian Tradition and the Theory of Absolute Monarchy," *English Historical Review* 79 (October 1964):747–60, and his "Filmer's Patriarchical History," *Historical Journal* 9, no. 2 (1960):157–71. It is clear that not all of those who have come to share a higher estimate of James I's general achievement would want to align themselves with Greenleaf's interpretation of the period. See, e.g., Conrad Russell, *Parliaments and English Politics, 1621–1629* (Oxford, 1979).

9. Greenleaf, *Order, Empiricism, and Politics*, 61.

10. Dr. John Cowell, *A Law Dictionary or Interpreter of Words and Terms Used Either in the Common or Statute Laws* (Cambridge, Eng., 1607); see esp. *in v.* King and Prerogative. For the reception this work received and for its subsequent fate, see McIlwain, ed., *Political Works of James I,* lxxxvii–lxxxix.

11. "A Speach to the Lords and Commons of the Parliament at White-Hall, . . . Anno 1609," in McIlwain, ed., *Political Works of James I,* 307–8.

12. Greenleaf, "Thomasian Tradition," 748 (a particularly succinct statement). Cf. his "James I and the Divine Right of Kings," 38n1 and 39–44, and *Order, Empiricism, and Politics,* 60–67 and 14–15, where he properly concedes that F. D. Wormuth's oddly neglected little book, *The Royal Prerogative, 1603–1649* (Ithaca, 1939), esp. 6–8, 44, 69–70, constitutes something of an exception because of the degree of attention it pays to "the political theory of order." Tillyard's influential book was first published in 1943.

13. Greenleaf, "James I and the Divine Right of Kings," 39–40; *Order, Empiricism, and Politics,* 15–17.

14. Greenleaf, "Thomasian Tradition," 748.

15. Greenleaf, "James I and the Divine Right of Kings," 38; *Order, Empiricism, and Politics,* 67.

16. This is the dating of Filmer's book argued for by James Daly, *Sir Robert Filmer and English Political Thought* (Toronto, 1979), 4–5.

17. Greenleaf, "Thomasian Tradition," 747, 757.

18. Ibid., 759, referring to Thomas Hobbes, *Leviathan,* ed. Michael Oakeshott (Oxford, 1946), 173.

19. Daly, *Sir Robert Filmer;* Daly, "The Idea of Absolute Monarchy in Seventeenth-Century England," *Historical Journal* 21, no. 2 (1978):227–50; Daly, *Cosmic Harmony and Political Thinking in Early Stuart England,* Transactions of the American Philosophical Society, n.s., 79, pt. 7 (Philadelphia, 1979).

20. Daly, *Cosmic Harmony,* 5n1. Daly also stresses the alignment

between *artificial* and *imposed* when he later discusses (33 and n. 6) the views of the English Puritans, views that he sees as profoundly at odds with the vision of cosmic harmony.

21. Daly, *Cosmic Harmony*, 22.

22. Ibid.

23. Ibid., 22 and 27, citing William Falkner, *Christian Loyalty* (London, 1679), 10–11.

24. Daly, *Cosmic Harmony*, 29, referring to Greenleaf, *Order, Empiricism, and Politics*, 8–9, 41, 47–48, 56, 94, 109, 187, and Greenleaf, "Thomasian Tradition," 747–48. Note that Robert Eccleshall, *Order and Reason in Politics: Theories of Absolute and Limited Monarchy in Early Modern England* (Oxford, 1978), 5, 9–16, mounts on somewhat different grounds another challenge to Greenleaf's assumption that early-modern notions of limited monarchy are to be linked not with the "traditional," Lovejoyesque "world view of order," but with "a novel empiricist style of thinking."

25. Daly sets forth the line of argument reproduced above in his "Idea of Absolute Monarchy," 227–50.

26. Daly, *Cosmic Harmony*, 29.

27. Richard Hooker, *Of the Laws of Ecclesiastical Polity*, I, ii, 6, ed. Christopher Morris, 2 vols. (London, 1958), 1:154; cited in Daly, *Cosmic Harmony*, 22.

28. Hooker, *Of the Laws of Ecclesiastical Polity*, I, ii, 2 and 6, ed. Morris, 1:150 and 154.

29. Filmer, *Patriarcha*, chap. 24, in *Patriarcha and Other Political Works of Sir Robert Filmer*, ed. Peter Laslett (Oxford, 1949), 103.

30. James I, "A Speach to the Lords and Commons," in *Political Works of James I*, ed. McIlwain, 308–10.

31. James I, "A Speach in the Starre-Chamber . . . Anno 1616," in *Political Works of James I*, ed. McIlwain, 333.

32. See his letter to the judges in the case of *commendams* in which, evoking "our absolute authoritie royall," he lectured them to the effect that "his Majestie had a doble prerogative, whereof the one was ordinary, and had relacion to his private interest, which mought bee, and was, every day disputed in Westminster Hall. The other [the absolute] was of a higher nature, referringe to his supreame and imperiall power and soveragntie, which ought not to bee disputed or handled in vulgar argument" (*Acts of the Privy Council of England, 1615–16* [London, 1925], 601).

33. For these references (and others) to invocations of the distinction between the two powers in the English legal and political literature of the fifteenth, sixteenth, and seventeenth centuries, see Francis Oakley, "Jacobean Political Theology: The Absolute and Ordinary

Powers of the King," *Journal of the History of Ideas* 29, no. 3 (1968): 323–25.

34. Daly, "Idea of Absolute Monarchy," 232. He does not mention it in *Cosmic Harmony*. Nor, despite his discussion of the "world view of order," is there any clear reference to the distinction in Eccleshall, *Order and Reason*.

35. For a happy exception to this generalization, see now Corinne Comstock Weston and Janelle Renfrow Greenberg, *Subjects and Sovereigns: The Grand Controversy over Legal Sovereignty in Stuart England* (Cambridge, Eng., 1981), esp. 10–18.

36. Geoffrey R. Elton, *England under the Tudors* (London, 1959), 402–3.

37. R. F. V. Heuston, *Essays in Constitutional Law*, 2d ed. (London, 1964), 62.

38. John W. Allen, *English Political Thought: 1603–1660* (London, 1938), 16.

39. F. W. Maitland, *The Constitutional History of England* (Cambridge, Eng., 1920), 258.

40. William S. Holdsworth, *A History of English Law*, 16 vols. (London, 1922–66), 4:202, 206–7; 6:20–22; cf. 2:596–97.

41. Charles H. McIlwain, *Constitutionalism: Ancient and Modern*, rev. ed. (Ithaca, 1947), 67–130.

42. Margaret A. Judson, *The Crisis of the Constitution: An Essay in Constitutional and Political Thought in England, 1603–1645* (New Brunswick, N.J., 1949), 25ff., 111ff.; Heuston, *Essays in Constitutional Law*, 61–62; Francis D. Wormuth, *The Origins of Modern Constitutionalism* (New York, 1949), 34–39; perhaps also George L. Mosse, *The Struggle for Sovereignty in England from the Reign of Queen Elizabeth to the Petition of Right* (East Lansing, Mich., 1950), esp. 50–51, 76–78, 81–84.

43. Ewart Lewis, "King above Law? 'Quod Principi Placuit' in Bracton," *Speculum* 39 (1964):266; Brian Tierney, "Bracton on Government," ibid., 38 (1963):295–317; Fritz Schulz, "Bracton on Kingship," *English Historical Review* 60 (May 1945):172; Wiebke Fesefeldt, *Englische Staatstheorie des 13. Jahrhunderts: Henry de Bracton und sein Werk* (Göttingen, 1962), 73–74n84; Gaines Post, "Bracton on Kingship," *Tulane Law Review* 42 (1968):545.

44. See George Mendenhall, *Law and Covenant in Israel and the Ancient Near East* (Pittsburgh, 1955); Delbert R. Hillers, *Covenant: The History of a Biblical Idea* (Baltimore, 1969).

45. Aegidius Romanus, *De ecclesiastica potestate*, III, caps. 2, 3, 7, 9, ed. Richard Scholz (Weimar, 1929), 149–50, 152, 156–59, 181–82, 190–94; John Duns Scotus, *Oxoniense scriptum in librum primum*

Sententiarum Magistri Petri Lombardi (Coimbra, 1609), I, dist. 44, qu. unica, 677–78; *Guillelmi de Ockham: Quodlibeta septem, Quodl.* VI, qu. 1, ed. Joseph C. Wey, *Opera theologica* 9 of *Guillelmi de Ockham: Opera philosophica et theologica ad fidem codicem manuscriptorum edita* (St. Bonaventure, N.Y.: Franciscan Institute, 1980), 586; Pierre d'Ailly, *Quaestiones super I, III, et IV Sententiarum* (Lyons, 1500), I, qu. 9, art. 2 M, fol. 120r; John Major, *In primum Sententiarum* (Paris, 1510), I, dist. 44, qu. 1, fol. ci v.

46. Walter Charleton, *The Darknes of Atheism Dispelled by the Light of Nature: A Physico-theologicall Treatise* (London, 1652), chap. 4, sec. 5, p. 136, where he assures us that "though God hath by the severe laws of Nature bound up the hands of his Creatures . . . , yet he has reserved his own freedom, and as an absolute Monarch can at pleasure alter, transcend, or pervert those Statutes, and give a new Commission to his Ministers to work by a new way, in order to the causation of any extraordinary effect. . . ." Cf. ibid., 125. Descartes to Mersenne, April 15, 1630, in *Oeuvres de Descartes,* ed. Charles Adam and Paul Tannery, 13 vols. (Paris, 1897–1910), 1:145.

47. Sir John Davies, *The Question Concerning Impositions, Tonnage, Poundage* . . . (London, 1656), 30–32. The work was written ca. 1625.

48. Edward Forset, *A Comparative Discourse of the Bodies Natural and Politique* (London, 1606), 20–21, where he continues: ". . . which (besides that which is regular in regiment, and from his power and goodnes imparted unto the people) hath still, and reteineth to it selfe certaine prerogative rights of most ample extensions, and most free exemptions, whereof true reverence (filled with all submissive acknowledgments and contented with that portion and interest which it receiveth from regalitie) admitteth no questioning disputes . . ."

49. For the pertinent references, see Oakley, "Jacobean Political Theology," 325 and 329. For the use of the distinction in relation to the powers of the fifteenth-century Hungarian monarchs, see Joseph Holub, "Ordinaria potentia—absoluta potentia," *Revue historique de droit français et étranger,* 4th ser., 28, no. 1 (1950):92–99.

50. Jean Bodin, *De republica: Libri sex* (Ursellis, 1601), 135 and 160, and in the English translation, *The Six Bookes of a Commonweale, Out of the French and Latin Copies Done into English by Richard Knolles* (London, 1606), 92 and 109. The reference to Innocent IV does not occur in the text of the French version. Cf. Innocent IV, *Apparatus super libros decretalium* (Venice, 1481), *ad* X, 1, 6, 20 *in v.* Ordinationem (no foliation).

51. Hostiensis (Henricus de Segusia), *Lectura in Quinque Decretalium Gregorianarum Libros* (Paris, 1512), *ad* X, 5, 31, 8 *in v.* Ita,

and *ad* X, 3, 35, 6 *in v.* Nec summus pontifex, fols. LXXIr and CXXXr; Johannes Andreae, *In tertium Decretalium librum Novella Commentaria* (Venice, 1581), *ad* X, 3, 35, 6, fol. 179v, §28.

52. See the works cited in Oakley, "Jacobean Political Theology," esp. 329–33, to which I would now add Jacques Almain, *Exposito circa decisiones Magistri Guilelmi Occam super potestate ecclesiastica et laica,* in Jean Gerson, *Opera omnia,* ed. Louis Ellies Dupin, 5 vols. (Antwerp, 1706), 2:1091–92, 1095, and Almain, *De dominio naturali, civili et ecclesiastico,* in ibid., 2:968. For Henry of Ghent, see the text in John Marrone, "The Absolute and Ordained Powers of the Pope: An Unedited Text of Henry of Ghent," *Mediaeval Studies* 36 (1974):23–27; and the canonistic texts of Panormitanus cited in K. W. Nörr, *Kirche und Konzil bei Nicolaus de Tudeschis* (Cologne, 1964), 47–49, 51.

53. See texts cited above, n. 51. Gratian included St. Jerome's words at C. 32, qu. 5, c. 11, in *Corpus Juris Canonici,* ed. Aemilius Friedberg, 2 vols. (Leipzig, 1879–81), 1:1135.

54. Aegidius Romanus, *De ecclesiastica potestate,* lib. IV, cap. 7, ed. Scholz, pp. 181–82.

55. Summarizing here ibid., lib. III, caps. 2, 3, and 9, pp. 149–50, 190–95. (The references to Daniel 3:20f. occur at 158 and 192.)

56. *Appelation deutscher Geistlichen von dem Executor des vom Papste geforderten Zehntens an den päpstlichen Stuhl (1352–60),* in *Acta Imperii Inedita,* ed. Edward Winkelmann, 2 vols. (Innsbruck, 1885), 2:843 (no. 1182). Cf. Augustin Renaudet, *Préreforme et humanisme à Paris pendant les premières guerres d'Italie: 1494–1517* (Paris, 1916), 201–2 and esp. 202n3, for the important speech of the royal advocate Lemaistre in February 1487/8, which employs the distinction to defend the liberties of the Gallican church.

57. See Winkelmann, ed., *Acta Imperii Inedita,* 2:843 (no. 1182).

58. See above, chaps. 2 and 3, pp. 60–61, 73–74.

59. For some further observations on this point, see Oakley, "Jacobean Political Theology," 339–46.

60. Marrone, "Absolute and Ordained Powers," 21. Marrone notes (17–18) that Henry also rejected the application of the distinction to God because it would suggest that of his absolute power he could act unjustly.

61. See Georges Weill, *Les Théories sur le pouvoir royal en France pendant les guerres de religion* (Paris, 1891), 153, where he cites the pertinent passage from Lambert Daneau's *Ethices christianae liber secundus* (1577); Rycharde Taverner, *The Garden of Wysedome* (London, 1539), Sig. Di r-v.

62. Hugh of St. Victor, *De sacramentis christianae fidei,* I, 2, cap. 8, in *Patrologiae Cursus Completus . . . ,* Series Latina, ed. J.-P. Migne,

221 vols. (Paris, 1844–), 176:237; Peter Lombard, *In libros sententiarum,* I, dist. 45, in ibid. 192:642–44; Thomas Aquinas, *Summa theologiae,* Ia, qu. 19, art. 11; *Guillelmi de Ockham: Scriptum in Librum Primum Sententiarum Ordinatio,* dist. 46, qu. 1, ed. Giraldus I. Etzkorn and Franciscus E. Kelley, *Opera theologica* 4 (1979):670–75; for Luther see the pertinent citations and extensive discussion in John Dillenberger, *God Hidden and Revealed: The Interpretation of Luther's Deus Absconditus and Its Significance for Religious Thought* (Philadelphia, 1953), 6–8, 109, 139–40; William Ames, *The Marrow of Sacred Divinity,* bk. I, chap. 7, in *The Marrow of Theology,* ed. John D. Eusden, (Boston, 1968), 100; Walter Charleton, *The Darknes of Atheism Dispelled by the Light of Nature: A Physico-theological Treatise* (London, 1652), 352–54; Thomas Hobbes, *The Questions Concerning Liberty, Necessity, and Chance. Clearly Stated and Debated Between Dr. Bramhall Bishop of Derry, and Thomas Hobbes of Malmesbury* (London, 1656), 10–11, 78–79. In the paragraphs that follow I draw upon the line of argument pursued in Francis Oakley, "The 'Hidden' and 'Revealed' Wills of James I: More Political Theology," *Studia Gratiana* 15 (1972):363–75.

63. For these correspondences, see the texts referred to above in n. 62 and also William Perkins, *Treatise of God's Free Grace and Man's Free-will,* in *The Workes of That Famous and Worthie Minister of Christ . . . M. W. Perkins,* 3 vols. (Cambridge, 1608), 1:704, col. 2A–B; Samuel Rutherford, *Lex Rex: The Law and the Prince* (London, 1644), 71; Edward Fowler, *The Principles and Practices of Certain Moderate Divines of the Church of England Abusively Called Latitudinarians* (London, 1671), 201–6; John Norton, *The Orthodox Evangelist* (London, 1654), 91–2; John Wallis, *A Brief and Easie Explanation of the Shorter Catechism* (London, 1662), Table I, sig. E 4.

64. In Perkins, *Workes,* 1:704, col. 2A–B.

65. The texts are cited above, pp. 96–98, 104–5.

66. Though historians have sometimes confused this distinction with that between the *potentia dei absoluta/ordinata;* see, e.g., J. B. Korolec, "Free Will and Free Choice," in *The Cambridge History of Later Medieval Philosophy,* ed. Norman Kretzmann, Anthony Kenny, and Jan Pinborg (Cambridge, Eng., 1982), 639–40. But see also Heiko A. Oberman, *The Harvest of Medieval Theology: Gabriel Biel and Late Medieval Nominalism* (Cambridge, Mass., 1963), 476, 103–4. Cf. Johannes Altenstaig, *Vocabularius Theologie complectens vocabulorum descriptiones, diffinitiones et significatus ad theologiam utilium . . .* (Mindesheim, 1517), fols. CCLXXVI v–CCLXXII r.

67. Charleton, *Darknes of Atheisme,* 354: "Since, therefore, it is impossible for us to make ourselves privy to the *concealed will* of our

Creator, all that remains on our part is to endeavor, with all humility
and serenity, to conforme and cooperate to his *Revealed.*" Cf. Hobbes,
Questions Concerning Liberty, Necessity, and Chance, 10–11.

68. Balthasar Hübmaier, *Das andere Büchlein von der Freiwillig-
keit des Menschen,* pt. III, in *Schriften,* ed. Gunnar Westin and Torsten
Bergsten, Quellen u. Forschungen zur Reformationsgeschichte 29
(Heidelberg, 1962), 416–18. I quote from the translation of the pertinent
passages included in George H. Williams, ed., *Spiritual and Anabaptist
Writers,* Library of Christian Classics 25 (Philadelphia, 1957), 132–34.

69. And as such, therefore, "properly made by the King onely."

70. Cf. Hübmaier's contrast of the will (and justice) of God with the
will (and mercy) of Christ: "Paul spoke clearly and plainly of this distinction of the two wills [hidden and revealed] when he said (I *Cor.*
2:16): Who hath known the mind of the Lord? But we have the mind of
Christ. When Paul writes: Who has known the mind of the Lord? he
refers to the hidden will of God, just as Isaiah (ch. 45:15) calls our God a
hidden God. When Paul says: We have Christ's mind, he refers to the
revealed and preached will of God, who was God himself, and became
man." (Williams, ed., *Spiritual and Anabaptist Writers,* 133; *Schriften,*
ed. Westin and Bergsten, 417).

71. James I, "A Speach to the Lords and Commons of the Parliament at White-Hall, . . . Anno 1609," in *Political Works of James I,* ed.
McIlwain, 308.

Epilogue

1. Both of which resonate powerfully to the notion of sovereign will
that was central to the covenantal tradition: legal positivism by identifying the legislating will as the constitutive moment of law, consent
theory by its grounding of political obligation in the autonomous wills
of a concatenation of praeter-political individuals. For some thoughts
on the former, see Francis Oakley, "Medieval Theories of Natural Law:
William of Ockham and the Significance of the Voluntarist Tradition,"
Natural Law Forum 6 (1961):65–83. And on the latter, Oakley, "Legitimation by Consent: The Medieval Roots," *Viator* 14 (1983):303–35.

2. Arthur O. Lovejoy, *The Great Chain of Being: A Study in the
History of an Idea* (Cambridge, Mass., 1936), 3.

3. Bhikhu Parekh and R. N. Berki, "The History of Political Ideas: A
Critique of Q. Skinner," *Journal of the History of Ideas* 24, no. 2
(1973):183 (italics in the original), where the authors properly stress the
importance of the division of labor among intellectual historians.

4. The anguished Thomist reaction to Lovejoy's treatment of Aquinas in *Great Chain of Being* and the lively (if protracted) skirmish that ensued together provide a classic illustration of this phenomenon. See A. C. Pegis, *Saint Thomas and the Greeks* (Milwaukee, 1939), esp. 21ff.; H. Veatch, "A Note on the Metaphysical Grounds for Freedom, with Special Reference to Professor Lovejoy's Thesis in 'The Great Chain of Being,'" *Philosophy and Phenomenological Research* 7, no. 3 (1947):391–412, with Lovejoy's reply at 413–38, Veatch's response, ibid., no. 4:622–25, and Lovejoy's rejoinder in ibid., 625–34; A. C. Pegis, "*Principale Volitum:* Some Notes on a Supposed Thomistic Contradiction," ibid., 9, no. 1 (1948):51–70; Lovejoy, "Necessity and Self-Sufficiency in Thomistic Theology: A Reply to President Pegis," ibid., 71–88, with Pegis's reply at 89–97; Lovejoy, "Comment on Mr. Pegis's Rejoinder," ibid., no. 2:284–90, with Pegis's further reply in ibid., 291–93.

5. Endorsing here the view stated by Parekh and Berki, "History of Political Ideas," 182–84, though not necessarily all of the claims they choose to affiliate with that view.

6. See Michael Oakeshott, Introduction to his edition of Thomas Hobbes, *Leviathan* (Oxford, 1940), xi–xiii. Cf. the pertinent comments of John Gunnell, *Political Theory: Tradition and Interpretation* (Cambridge, Mass., 1979), 80, and Andrew Lockyer, "'Traditions' as Context in the History of Political Theory," *Political Studies* 27, no. 2 (1979):203. The "traditions" that W. H. Greenleaf (*Order, Empiricism, and Politics: Two Traditions of English Political Thought, 1500–1700* [London, 1964]) makes the subject of his own inquiry are much more clearly historical.

7. For this distinction between "traditions of discourse" and "traditions of thought" and in much of what follows I am indebted to Lockyer's thoughtful argument in his "'Traditions' as Context."

8. Lockyer, "'Traditions' as Context," 216. Note that Quentin Skinner, *pace* the criticisms of Parekh and Berki (and despite his own reservations about the success of Greenleaf's attempt to write the history of political thought in terms of dominant traditions), has been more than willing to concede that his own "attempt to focus on the conventions of political argument obviously tends to culminate in a study of *genres* and traditions of discourse" ("Some Problems in the Analysis of Political Thought and Action," *Political Theory* 2, no. 3 (1974):287–88.

9. In Skinner's terms, the meaning he intended, the illocutionary force of his utterances. See R. G. Collingwood, *An Autobiography* (Oxford, 1939), esp. 29–43, and *An Essay on Metaphysics* (Oxford, 1940), esp. 21–33.

Index

Lovejoy, Arthur (*cont.*)
literature, 33–34; and Aquinas, 55;
criticism of, 129–30; and God,
44–48; and history of ideas, 34–38;
and intellectual history, 9–10; and
methodology, 32–40; and Plato, 36,
37; "Reflections," 131; and Skinner, 30–31; unit-ideas, 35–38, 39
Luther, Martin, 51, 57, 82, 115

McIlwain, Charles Howard, 95, 107,
108, 111
Maier, Anneliese, 146
Major, John, 82, 108
Marrow of Sacred Divinity, The
(Ames), 51, 58
Marsilius of Inghen, 83
Mather, Increase, 59
Medulla theologica (Ames), 51
Meinecke, Friedrich, 20
Methodology: and history of ideas,
28–31; and Lovejoy, 32–40; Weber
on, 15
Miller, Perry, 20
Miracles, 89
Monarchy, absolute, 93–118
Moral law, 81
More, Henry, 91, 150
More, Sir Thomas, 61
Mots et les choses, Les (Foucault), 23

Natural law, 82–92
Nebuchadnezzar, 57, 59, 74, 83, 111
New Criticism, 30–31, 33, 34
Newton, Sir Isaac, 70, 72, 74, 85, 87,
89, 92; *Principia*, 90
Nicholas of Autrecourt, 78–79, 84
Nietzsche, Friedrich, 24
Nominalists and moral law, 81
Norton, John, 59
Nun's Priest's Tale (Chaucer), 64

Oakeshott, Michael, 121
Oberman, Heiko A., 145
Ockham, William of, 46, 51, 52–53,

56, 60, 61, 63, 64, 79, 86, 108, 115,
137; and moral laws, 81; and natu-
ral law, 83; and voluntarist posi-
tion, 145
Odovacar, 41
Order of Things, The (Foucault), 24
"Ordinary," 106
Orthodox Evengelist (Norton), 59

Paris theologians, 54
Passerin d'Entrèves, 20
Passmore, John, 31
Patriarcha . . . (Filmer), 95, 99
Perkins, William, 115
Plato, 20, 36, 37, 45, 46
Plotinus, 37
Pocock, J. G. A., 28, 39, 40
Pope and absolute power, 110–11,
113, 114
Poststructuralists, 25–26, 27

Ranke, Leopold von, 130
Ray, John, 90
Reformation, Protestant, 60
Religion and science, 67–92
Republic (Plato), 36
Rome, 41–42

Saussure, Ferdinand de, 24
Schelling, Friedrich, 38
Science and theology, 67–92
Searle, John, 28
Shapin, Steven, 151
Shepherd, Thomas, 59
Skinner, Quentin, 28–29, 38, 40; and
Lovejoy, 30–31, 32, 34, 129–30;
and traditions of discourse, 159
Spinoza, Baruch, 37, 46
Stone, Lawrence, 18, 19, 127
Structuralism, 127
Stubbe, Henry, 70
Sturm, Johann Christoph, 91, 92
Suárez, Francisco, 51, 57–59, 82, 88
Summa theologiae (Aquinas), 49
Sydenham, Thomas, 148

Library of Congress Cataloging in Publication Data

Oakley, Francis.
   Omnipotence, covenant, and order.

   Includes bibliographical references and index.
      1. Philosophy—History.   2. History—Philosophy—
History.   3. Lovejoy, Arthur O. (Arthur Oncken),
1873–1962.   I. Title.
B72.017 1984   190   83-45945
ISBN 0-8014-1631-0 (alk. paper)